T. Campbell

The China review

Notes and queries on the Far East

T. Campbell

The China review
Notes and queries on the Far East

ISBN/EAN: 9783741172489

Manufactured in Europe, USA, Canada, Australia, Japa

Cover: Foto ©Thomas Meinert / pixelio.de

Manufactured and distributed by brebook publishing software
(www.brebook.com)

T. Campbell

The China review

Vol. V.   No. 4.

TH

CHINA REVIEW:

OR

NOTES AND QUERIES ON THE FAR EAST.

PUBLISHED EVERY TWO MONTHS.

JANUARY AND FEBRUARY, 1877

HONGKONG
"CHINA MAIL" OFFICE, No. 2, WYNDHAM STREET.

AGENTS:
TRÜBNER, SMITH & WALSH
LONDON TRÜBNER & Co., 57 & 59, LUDGATE HILL.

Price $6 50 per Annum

CONTENTS OF No. 4.

ESSAYS ON THE CHINESE LANGUAGE.

(Continued from page 152.)

CHAPTER V.

Chinese Use of Metaphor.

Instinctive cries and vocal imitations are at most the material of which human speech is made. They may actually be formed into articulate rational utterances, but in themselves they lack the necessary quality for constituting them human speech. Both they and the mute bodily gestures before described act rather as aids and way-preparers for articulate language. This last must in the beginning of man's history have been very scanty, and must have needed all the helps which art and nature could yield. It is not improbable that all human speech had its physical origin—its apparent source—in vocal utterances which only suggested or recalled the sounds of nature. "Le langage primitif," says Renan, "fut donc le produit commun de l'esprit et du monde : envisagé dans sa forme, il était l' expression de la raison pure ; envisagé dans sa matière, il n'était que le reflet de la vie sensible. Ceux qui ont tiré le langage exclusivement de la sensation se sont trompés, aussi bien que ceux qui ont assigné aux idées une origine purement matérielle. La sensation a fourni l'élément variable et accidentel, qui aurait pu être tout autrement qu'il n'est, c'est-à-dire les mots ; mais la forme rationelle, sans laquelle les *mots* n'auraient point été une *langue*, en d'autres termes la grammaire, tel est l'élément pur et transcendant qui donne à l'œuvre un caractère vraiment humain."[*] In order to change the instinctive and other utterances above mentioned into human speech there were needed the alchemy of reason, and the exercise of man's fancy and imagination. Only by the working of these could those sounds come to serve as a means of communication among men and attain the dignity of rational speech. Hence, as has been often said, a people's language is everywhere a sure evidence—the barometer, as a well-known work expresses it—of their intellectual progress and the degree of culture to which they have attained. "Certainly," says Bacon, "words are the footsteps of reason and the footsteps tell something about the body."[†] They tell us indeed the history of reason—of the successive steps by which man rises from the mere observing the facts of nature and roughly guessing at their analogies to the grandest deductions which he has elaborated. Locke and others after him have pointed out how all our

[*] *De l'Origine du Langage,* p. 122. See also Farrar, *Chapters on Language,* p. 182.
[†] Works (Ed. Ellis & Spedding), Vol. IV. p. 441.

terms for spiritual ideas originated in expressions for physical sensations, or, as Locke phrases it, are "ultimately derived from such as signify sensible Ideas."[*] But in languages like our own the traces of the process are often obscured by the wear and tear of time, by the influence of transplanted terms, or by other agencies. Jean Paul, accordingly, speaks truly when he says that "every language is in respect to spiritual relations a dictionary of faded metaphors."[†] To take a homely instance, the opposition between sense and nonsense now is very different from that which was in the mind of a pious quaint old poet who little more than two hundred years ago wrote—

"Frogs marry fish and flesh; bats, bird and beast;
Sponges, nonsense and sense; mines, th' earth and plants."

Many languages, however, retain the use of metaphor with little or no disguise. The name for the physical act or effect is thus the name for the mental or emotional operation, and the only means for its expression. In other languages there is often parallel to this direct use of it a more refined less materialistic use of metaphor. Hebrew, for example, has for many purely mental and emotional acts and states only sensuous expressions.[‡] The Chinese language, on the other hand, has often for spiritual phenomena along with the terms immediately derived from sensible ideas others which are at least more remotely so derived.

It will help us much in gaining an insight into the nature and qualities of this language if we try to find out what use it makes of metaphor. In the present essay, accordingly, an attempt is made to bring forward a few examples of its employment as illustrating Chinese modes of thinking

and speaking. These examples are taken not so much from classical and philosophical treatises as from popular literature and from the talk of the common people. Prémare has treated at some length the use of metaphor by good Chinese writers, and his observations on this subject as on all matters relating to this language are worthy a careful reading.[*]

"Metaphor," says Max Müller, "is one of the most powerful engines in the construction of human speech, and without it we can hardly imagine how any language could have progressed beyond the simplest rudiments. Metaphor generally means the transferring of a name from the object to which it properly belongs to other objects which strike the mind as in some way or other participating in the peculiarities of the first object." Further on he distinguishes two kinds of metaphor which he calls radical and poetical.[†]

In taking notice of some of the occasions on which the Chinese are wont to use metaphorical ways of speaking it will be convenient to begin with the expressions for those simple acts and states in which the interaction between mind and body is easily observed. These furnish us with examples of the transfer of the name for the outward physical phenomenon to the internal immaterial cause.

Thus to pout or sulk is expressed by several phrases, each, however, merely describing the bodily gesture. One of these is ku-tu-tsui (胍肚嘴), literally to belly or paunch the mouth. Another is pa-tsui-yi-liu (把嘴一咧), to make a long mouth; and a third is chui-tsui-p'eng-sai (嘬嘴膨腮), to pout the lips and inflate the cheeks.[‡]

To look for long and eagerly as a mother watching for a truant child or a wife for her tarrying husband is expressed by such

---

* Essay &c., Book III. Ch. 1.
† See Gerber's Die Sprache als Kunst, B. 1. S. 361.
‡ Renan, Histoire des Langues Semitiques, p. 22 &c. (4th Edn.); De l'Origine du Langage, p. 124 &c.

* Notitia Linguæ Sinicæ, p. 241, &c.
† Lectures on the Science of Language, Vol. 2, pp. 385 & 388 (6th Edn.).
‡ So in Foochow ch'ui-ta-t'u, puffed-out mouth, means pouting and sulking.

phrases as *wang-yen-yü-ch'uan* (望眼
欲穿), that is, gazing until the eyes are
becoming pierced. The meaning is that the
"eye-strings are being strained so as to en-
danger the falling out of the pupil." This
reminds us of the impatient words of the
desolate Imogen:

"I would have broke mine eye-strings;
cracked them but
To look upon him."

To become angry has various expressions,
most of which are derived from the physical
change seen or supposed to accompany the
internal emotion. Thus it is *shĕng-ch'i*
(生氣), to generate air or vapour, though
this is perhaps often a mere name for what
the Chinese think actually takes place. It
is also *fa-hung* (發紅), that is simply, to
redden, an expression used also for blushing.
Another term in common use is *fan-mien*
(番面), to change countenance or face.
But strong violent rage, indignation at some
atrocious deed, is expressed by *fa-chih* (髮
指), that is hair-finger, meaning that the
hair bristled up and stood on end.

Envy and jealousy are denoted by various
figures. A wife who is jealous is said to
take vinegar (*chi-tsu* 吃醋), whereas we
ascribe green eyes to jealousy the Chinese
speak of a person who is jealous or envious
as having red eyes, and *yen-hung-liao*
(眼紅了) is used where we would say
became envious. The redness is supposed
to be the result of internal heat, and another
common term for being envious is to have
the eyes hot (*yen-je* 眼熱). So to long for
or covet improperly what belongs to another
is to have eyes black for it, *yen-ch'ing-hei*
(眼晴黑). But for this last emotion
there are also other and stronger expressions. Such is the vulgar Mandarin phrase
han-la-tzŭ, or more fully *liu-han-la-tzŭ*, to
have the mouth watering for something, often applied to children wanting something
which they cannot obtain. A more elegant
expression though occurring also in popular
literature is *yen-yen* (涎嚥) with the
same meaning. *Yen-k'ung-yen* (涎空

嚥) is to long for or covet in vain, and
ch'ui-yen-Chin-ting (垂延晉鼎), to
water in the mouth for the Chin throne, has
long been a proverbial expression.

Women, as we have seen, use the gesture
of scraping their cheeks with their fingers
to signify loss of character or shamelessness.
From this is derived the expression *kuah-
mien* (刮面), which, like the Latin *per-
fricare os* (or *faciem*), means to put off or
lose all shame, and it is applied as well to
men as to women. Similar meanings are
attached to such common and obvious expressions as *tiu-lien* (丟臉), to lose face;
p'i-lien (皮臉), skin (or leather) face;
hou-lien-p'i (厚臉皮), or thick face
skin. The words *lien* (臉) and *mien* (面)
are constantly used on occasions on which
we would employ such words as reputation,
prestige, or character, as well as countenance
or expression of face. Thus a cold formal
look is a face covered with hoar-frost *man-
mien-shang-shuang* (滿面上霜) a freez-
ing expression. To have a good reputation
is to have a white face *pai-mien* (白面)
or simply to have a face.

The emotion of fear in its various degrees
has very many terms and phrases. It is
p'a (怕), simply to fear, the sound being
perhaps derived from the pa-pa, or pit-pat
of the heart agitated with alarm. It is
ching (驚), to shy, as a horse; *chü* (懼), to
flutter with fear, as a bird. But these three
terms have in common use for the most part
forgot their sensuous origin. Other less
abstract expressions are *chih-yi-liang* (吃
一喸),* to eat a shudder, that is to become greatly alarmed. The idea of cold is
brought out in such phrases as *han-sin* (寒
心), to be cold at heart, and *han-mao-tu-
k'ai-liao* (寒毛都開了), to bristle
up with a cold shudder. This idea of the
hair bristling up with great fear is also expressed by *fa-mao* (發毛), to bristle, a
phrase constantly applied to persons who
live in daily dread of ghosts and other ima-

* The character 喸 is probably not correct.

ginary torments. To frighten one to death is to burst his gall, *p'o-tan* (破 膽) ; and to be faint hearted is to have a small gall, to be *hsiao-tan* (小 膽).

The seat of sympathy and affection and of the moral nature generally is most usually referred by the Chinese to the heart, the bowels, or to both. Hence their commonest expressions for deep intense emotions, such as love and sympathy, are intimately associated with these parts of the body; and indeed there can scarcely be said to be any others in ordinary use among them. To love fondly, as a mother loves her child, is *t'êng* (疼), to suffer pain, that is, in the inward parts. When a person loves another through weal and through woe, in absence as when present, he is said to keep him cherished in his abdomen, literally, in the cavity of his heart *sin-k'êng-shang-wên-ts'un* (心 坎 上 温 存). When a man distresses himself very much about a matter he is said to be rending his bowels *tuan-ch'ang-tzŭ* (斷 腸 子). This expression is also used to denote the fond fretting of a wife for her husband or a mother for her child. Another and still stronger expression for the yearning love of a mother for her child, specially for her distress for it when ill, is *pa-ch'ang-wa-tu* (扒 腸 挖 肚), to rend the bowels and tear out the stomach. Does not this recall the striking words of Jesus : "σπλαγχνίζομαι ἐπὶ τὸν ὄχλον," lamely translated by "I have compassion on the multitude ?"[*] A common but somewhat literary phrase for carrying compassion or sympathy into practice is *t'i-hsü* (體 恤), to embody pity.

To be cunning and always trying to practise sharp tricks is to have a long nose, *ch'ang-pi* (長 鼻), and in Foochow a man who has always his wits about him, who cannot be fooled, is said to have a nose longer than a table, *p'ei-tong-kwo-toh* (鼻 長 過 棹). Another term for an unprincipled man, always ready to take advantage of his neighbour, is *pai-pi-tzŭ* (白 鼻 子), or, white nose. But to say that a man's nose is

depressed *nàh-p'ei* (凹 鼻) is at Foochow to say that he is angry or sullen. A bad temper seems always to be indicated by the nose in China as in other countries, and hence such requests as, " sed ira cadat naso rugosaque sanna."

In several of the instances of the use of metaphor just brought forward the original and derived senses of the word are not kept distinct; and this is true of countless other cases besides those given above. The word *sin* (心), heart, for example, denotes not only the literal heart of flesh, but also moral character or nature, intention, and other spiritual qualities or properties, and one of these meanings is often found mixed up with another.[*] This confusion occurs in all languages perhaps, and is sometimes not without a certain force and quaintness. As an example of it in our own language we may take part of the description of "the common singing-men in Cathedral Churches" given by an old writer. He says "Their humanity is a legge to the Residencer, their learning a Chapter, for they learne it commonly before they read it, yet the old Hebrew names are little beholding to them, for they mis-call them worse than one another. Though they never expound the Scripture, they handle it much, and pollute the Gospell with two things, their Conversation and their thumbes. Upon worky-dayes they behave themselves at Prayers as at their Pots, for they swallow them down in an instant."[†] Because of this indistinctness or confusion of meaning which adheres to metaphor some have held that it is a sign of weakness and poverty of speech or invention. Such it may have been originally during the process of the formation of a language, but it is not so any longer except in a limited degree. It is used now partly from old habit, partly of necessity, and partly for the sake of force and clearness. It links together the very beginning of speech,—when

[*] *Mark*, Ch. VIII. v. 2.

[*] Compare *Die Sprache als Kunst*, B. I. S. 245.

[†] Earle's *Micro-cosmographie*, Ch. 30.

form and substance, spirit and matter, the concrete and the abstract were as yet undistinguished, and the highest state of cultivation to which speech attains. As clothes, to adopt Cicero's illustration, were first used for protection against cold, and now used not only for that purpose but also for ornament, so metaphor was first used to clothe the simple thought and feelings of man and has come to perform many other functions while still serving its original purpose. Its advantages have been recognised by Chinese writers, and, as has been often pointed out, the whole of one of the six divisions of characters is called *chia-chie* (假借) or borrowed, that is, metaphorical.* A recent writer contrasts it, *pi* (譬), with *chih* (直) or direct speaking, and declares in favour of the former as the better medium for conveying instruction.

Hence in popular discourses on the social virtues we generally find the figurative mode of speaking largely used. Instead of speaking of sages or striking events, rousing or urging a man or a people to heroic deeds and the practice of virtue, the Chinese moralist speaks of drumming them. So Shakspeare makes Cæsar say of Antony—

> " but, to confound such time,
> That drums him from his sport, and speaks as loud
> As his own state, and ours."

Does the teacher wish to enforce the duty of a family to live closely united together in harmony, he speaks of its members as bone and flesh, *ku-jou* (骨肉). A curse is pronounced against him who sunders these, that is, who divides parent and child, brother and brother, husband and wife; so also a common expression for brothers is hand and foot *shou-tsu* (手足). Instead of saying that all the members of a large family live together contentedly the Chinese are wont to say that they all mess from the same pot *t'ung-kuo-chih-fan* (同鍋吃飯). Some of the expressions in use for family relations are not a little curious. Thus at Foochow a

father is often called a bridge, *kieu* (橋).* A man's sons-in-law call themselves and are called his *tan-tiao-ti* (担桃的), or carrying coolies. Relatives who are very distant are called *kua-k'o-chih-ch'in* (瓜葛之親), *kua* and *k'o* being the names of widely-spreading plants like cucumber and a trailing bean. To have a slight connexion or far removed relationship is to have a *kua-k'o*, the rest of the phrase being understood. These two words are also used to denote numerous descendants, a widely-branching family.†

There is often a sort of poetic beauty in these transfers of ideas and modes of expression. Thus a fresh old age is expressed by *ts'ang-pai* (蒼白), that is, dark and white, the brown or black hair of manhood being intermixed with the white hairs of old age. We speak of being in the green leaf and Cleopatra even refers to her " salad days," meaning the time of early vigorous life even if " green " and inexperienced. Instead of *ts'ang-pai* the phrase *êr-mao* (二毛) or piebald—two-haired—is often used, and this comes down from the time of the Chow dynasty. In the Tso-chuan a sentence is found which has long been famous, *pu-chung-shang-pu-chin-êr-mao* (不重傷不禽二毛), he does not wound the wounded nor capture an old man. To be past one's prime, to be going out of date, is to be going down the bridge—*hsia-chiao* (下橋), a phrase which is often applied to women who have outlived their youthful charms. Again, when a man is very old and seen to be playing the last act of his life, it is said of him *lou-chin* (漏盡), the sands of life are for him all run out.

For setting forth the beauties of the human body, again, nature presents many points of comparison of which the poet and his fellow, the lover, have never failed to take advantage. Taking the eyes as an example, we find the Chinese novel-writer

---

* See e.g. Prémare's *Notitia* &c. e.c.

* See Maclay & Baldwin's Dictionary, p. 354.
† Examples of the use of this expression will be found in the Dictionaries of Morrison and Williams.

comparing the eyes of his heroine to the rippled lake of Autumn—*ch'iu-p'o* (秋 波), and this has come to be a recognised synonym for a young lady's eyes. We now only speak of a maid as having "deep dark" eyes, but Solomon once said his love's were "the fish-pools in Heshbon." The large clear eyes of children are also in China called pools of water, and it pleases a mother very much to have it said to her that her little boy's eyes are each *yi-wa-shui* (一 涯 水) or a pool of clear water.

But perhaps in no department of the Chinese language do we find metaphor prevail more generally than in that which embraces the study for and attainment of the literary degrees and all matters relating to learning. It is needless to repeat how eagerly literary honours are sought after—with what perseverance, often for life, the aspirants compete for them from period to period. They have often to fight not only with numbers and the difficulties of the absurd requirements of the examinations, but also with poverty, fortune, and bribery. We can learn much of this from phrases in common use. Thus the building set apart for the examinations is called the *chi-wei* (棘 闈) or thorny inclosure, from the forms and solemnities with which the process is fenced round.* The essays of the competitors are called *hêng-wên* (衡 文), that is weighed or opposing literary compositions. This word *hêng* has a further metaphorical application to learning, for *hêng-mên* (衡 門) denotes a poor sage's humble cottage, the door of which consists of pieces of timber.† This term is derived originally from the old classic poetry, and is scarcely colloquial. But it points to the simple life or indeed poverty of the professed student. In China, as in Ireland, "truelie learning goeth very bare" in some respects at least, as we may see from many common phrases. An old student is called a *shi-*

nien-ch'uang-hsia (十 年 窓 下), literally, ten years close to the window, that is, very poor and so having to make the most of daylight. The phrase then comes to mean simply a scholar or learned man. So *han-chu'ang* (寒 窓), cold window, is a poor student; and *t'ung-ch'uang* (同 窓), or fellow-windowers, denotes companions in learning or fellow-students. Another designation for a poor scholar is *pu-yi-chih-shi* (布 衣 之 士), or cotton-clothed scholar, a very common term and often shortened to the mere *pu-yi*. It denotes also a plain, solid scholar, and also a man of learning who does not take office but lives among the people in obscurity. The Chinese apply the term grinding through in a more dignified way than we do to the close long-continued application of a diligent student. *Mo-lien* (磨 鍊), to grind and refine, but *mo* is also used alone. So also the term *tu-yü* (蠹 魚), or book-worm, is given to one who is overmuch given to reading. It is the duty of all sages, and indeed of all who have wrought out for themselves a knowledge of old truth, to hand on or bequeath that knowledge to their children or successors. The doing of this is called *hsin-ch'uan* (薪 傳), literally the delivering over of firewood, or *hsin-tan* (箄)-*ch'uan*, giving over the firewood basket. The metaphor is taken from the poor simple mountain peasant who has only his faggot-basket to bequeath to his children, as the true sage has only his store of truth to leave to his posterity. For not to increase learning or enlarge wisdom but only to transmit the world-old body of doctrine is the duty and glory of all true philosophers from Confucius downwards. *

Rude and half-civilised peoples generally feel a stronger sense of relationship with nature than those which have reached a high degree of culture. The former, accordingly, find analogies and resemblances between animals or even inanimate objects and themselves to a greater extent than do the latter. Thus we see names of animals

---

* The expression is also written 棘 闈, and see Williams' Dictionary s.v.: p. 1048.
† See e.g. Legge's *She-King*, p. 207.

* Cf. Legge's *Ch. Classics*, Vol. 1., p. 37.

transferred to men and human qualities ascribed to the brute creature, and the influence of these transfers lasts through all the history of a people. In Chinese this is a fruitful source of metaphor, as it has been in, perhaps, all languages. We need not refer to the existence of such surnames as Horse, Bear, Sheep, Prune, Pine, which may in some cases have been first nicknames and gradually become recognised surnames. But we find that the various qualities and characters supposed to be characteristic of certain animals when observed to exist in men have led to the transfer of the animal's name to man. Thus a cruel, heartless person is a wolf, *tsai-lang* (豺狼), and Mencius says, not to rescue a drowning sister-in-law is to be a wolf.' Instead of saying that a man looked fiercely the Chinese commonly say that he looked tiger *hu-shih* (虎視), and this word *hu* or tiger is used in countless instances where cruelty or ferocity is indicated. To be overbearing and presumptuous is to take the airs of an eagle—to soar like one *chi-chang* (鴟張), with which we may compare what Sir Kay says of Gareth—

"Tut; he was tame and meek enow with me,
Till peacock'd up with Lancelot's noticing."

Several phases of Chinese social life are well brought out by this kind of figurative speech. Thus at Foochow brokers, land-agents, and go-betweens generally are called white ants, *pah-ngie* (白蟻), because they eat up all the profits of the business on which they are employed. But the common people everywhere style themselves *ants* when making petition to the mandarins. Again grain-weevils, *liang-tu* (糧蠹), is the nickname given to the agents employed to collect the grain contributions, men who in the discharge of their office plunder the people and defraud the Government. This same word *tu*, meaning grub or weevil, is applied also to heretical and wicked books which corrode the heart. An official often

in memorials to the Emperor and on other occasions calls himself an old horse, *nu-t'ai* (駑駘), meaning that he lacks ability and expertness.

On the other hand properties and attributes of man are transferred to the lower animals, to the vegetable world, and to lifeless nature, the analogy which led to the transfer being sometimes hard to trace. Mosses and lichens are spoken of as the rocks' hair, *shih-fa* (石髮), and the grass of the field is spoken of as its coarse hair, *mao* (毛). The earth has its pulse *mo* (脈), and its air *ch'i* (氣) or mystic power. Its soil is called its flesh, *t'u-jou* (土肉), which is said to be thin, that is, poor; or thick, that is rich. A pass or other place of political importance in a country is called its throat *yen-hou* (咽喉). Again analogies are often discovered among animals, or between animals and plants, or between these and inanimate objects. Hence have arisen many and curious expressions, the name of one object being transferred either wholly or in part to another. Thus a blister on the foot is a *chien* (繭), or silkworm's cocoon; and a coin on the toe is a fowl's eye *chi-yen* (鷄眼). A bat is a *fei-shu* (飛鼠) or flying-mouse (or rat), a flitter-mouse. We speak of the flowers of certain leguminous plants as being papilionaceous or butterfly shaped, and we extend the analogy to others, the Chinese gardeners calling the pansy *yang-hu-tie* (洋蝴蝶). The moon and the sun are said to bud *meng* (萌), and the snow flakes are flowers *hua* (花).

That kind of metaphor by which the part is made to represent the whole or the individual the species is very common in Chinese. Thus *ming* (名) or name stands for person or individual, as do also certain other terms. A *mên* (門) or door is used to mean a family, and also a sect or school whether in religion, philosophy, or any of the arts. Pork is the national flesh-food of the Chinese, and among at least the poorer classes the word *jou* (肉) or meat, without any prefix means pork, just as once in England by the

---

* Legge's *Mencius*, p. 183. Compare Herbert Spencer's Essays, Vol. 3, p. 105.

word flesh was meant only pig's flesh.[*] In some places in the north of China the street thieves who steal from one's person are called *pa-yen-tai-ti* (把煙代的), that is, pipe-pilferers, the pipe being the article easiest to steal. Military service is often spoken of as wolf-smoke *lang-yen* (狼煙), from the signal-cones used in time of war, wolf's excrement being burned in these to warn by its smoke of impending danger. Hence a soldier says that he had three years military service abroad by saying that he had three years wolf-smoke.

The examples given above of the use of metaphor by the Chinese—and these are only a few and not well chosen—may serve to show in some degree the strength and weakness of this way of expression. In some cases it causes the continuance of a vagueness and looseness of meaning, and gives stability to error, but on the other hand in very many instances it imparts force and vividness and leads to facility of conception. To people not disposed to think deeply nor accustomed to notice fine points of difference the physical result will best recall or denote the spiritual cause, and the transfer of a name will cause the transfer of much more. There is danger, however, lest the type cast the antitype into forgetfulness, and the image supplant the god. We seem to see this often in Chinese life and conse-

quently often mirrored in the language. Hence come the numerous and, in many cases, slightly related meanings of words. But we must guard against statements such as that of Farrar, when, relying on the authority of Benloew apparently, he writes:—"We encounter once more in Chinese the phenomenon which we have observed in Hebrew, in the number of different meanings possessed by the same root; a phenomenon not solely but *mainly* explicable by the influence of metaphor. For instance, *chou* means a book, a tree, great heats, aurora, and the loss of a wager,"[*] and so on with other examples. When we write the Chinese characters for the sound *chou* (*shu*) here given, we find that there are not two of them alike or indeed related. It is not "the same root" but different roots which have the meaning here given. 書 is a book; 樹 a tree; 暑 great heat; 曙 aurora; and 輸 is the loss of a wager. In our own language the words rite, wright, right, write, are sounded alike or nearly so, but their histories show that they have no connexion, and they are all differently written. But the Chinese characters for book, tree, etc., are not even pronounced alike. In mandarin they differ in tone, but in the dialects they present not only this difference but also others.

T. WATTERS.

* See Marsh's *Lectures on the English Language*, p. 169 (The Student's Manual Edition).

* *Chapters on Language*, p. 208. The characters for "Great heat" and "Aurora" are, as written above, evidently related.

DEER-STALKING IN CHINA

AND

SPORTING NOTES.

Having heard that deer abounded in the hills in the district of *Kien-teh* in *An-hui* and in the *Peng-tsik* and *Hu-kow* districts in *Kiang-si*, and having had evidence of their existence from the fact of native sports-men offering them for sale in the market—very seldom, it must be admitted—we de-cided to try and procure a specimen of this noble game, in the interests of natural history as well as for sport, two eminent naturalists having declared the deer in the above neighbourhood to be of a different kind to those found in Europe.* The Chi-nese hunters whom we had met stated they were too wild to procure with the inferior weapons, and as rewards had failed to bring forth specimens required by our naturalists, we made up our mind to try for ourselves, and with what success the reader will soon learn.

Deer-stalking in China is a novel sport to foreigners, and if we have entered into too minute details to interest the China reader, our excuse is that they may interest readers abroad unfamiliar with the manner in which shooting expeditions are conducted in this country. Let us therefore commence this narrative by giving a description of our excursion to the deer hills.

Most shooting trips in Central China are conducted in boats; that is, one travels from

place to place in yachts or 'house-boats, and our first journey to *Kien-teh*, for the greater part of the way, was no exception to this rule.

Our yacht having been sent down the Yangtsze some hundred and fifty miles or so on service work, we arranged that she should meet us at a certain place on her return trip; and to save time, went down by steamer to where we hoped to find the yacht. To afford more room on board we had hired a small native sailing craft to accommodate the coolies, cook, dogs and stores, &c., also to ensure getting up the creeks should there happen to be insufficient water for the yacht, as late in the autumn the creeks and affluents are very shallow. The journey to our place of rendezvous, about seventy miles, was accomplished in a few hours by the Yangtsze river steamer in which we took passage, and this saved us at least a day, or many more, had we sailed down and a head wind overtaken us. It was about an hour after sunset when we disembarked from the steamer, and our first disappointment was to find that the yacht had not yet arrived, the clear and calm weather having retarded her progress up stream. Fortunately there was room in the provision boat; but it was very uncomfortable, and we had brought few things with us, as the yacht was well found in all that was required in the way of bed-ding, crockery and other creature comforts. In anticipation, however, of such a contin-

* See Journal de mon Troisième Voyage d'Ex-ploration dans l'Empire Chinois, par M. l'Abbé Armand David, Vol. II., p. 121.

gency as missing the yacht, my companion, an old campaigner, had with laudable fore-thought sent some extra supplies in the native boat, so that if the yacht did not turn up the following morning we were pre-pared to start in the small mat-covered and deckless boat in which we passed the night, in company with nine natives, comprising the crew, servants, and our two dogs. It was a bright moonlight night, and for the time of the year—late in November—compa-ratively warm, so that in spite of the airiness of the boat and hardness of the bottom boards, which served us as bed, table, chairs, &c., we passed a fairly comfortable night. The Yangtsze having fallen very slowly that year, we found plenty of water in the *Kien-teh* river which empties into the Yang-tse at *Tung-lin*, and soon after entering the mouth we were sailing on the surface of a beautiful clear lake, which washes the base of the hills to the south-west for many miles round. After a pleasant sail of a few hours it became evident that we must keep to the channel of the still overflown river, for as we advanced, the banks gradually became visible from their long summer submersion, and finally quite defined and free from water. Both shores were swarming with wild geese and cranes, but our battery of fowling-pieces, rifles and duck-gun failed to bring down a single goose, although we seemed to be well within range when we opened fire from the boat as it sailed noiselessly along. We also saw several fine eagles swooping down upon the geese, and on more than one occasion they prevented our stealing a march on them, by flushing them before we got within range. In fact the heroic way in which the geese stood our volley of S.S.G. shot from a large-bore duck-gun led us to con-clude that they were armour-plated.

When about eight or ten miles from the Yangtsze, we left the soft green breadth of the lake behind us, and as we neared the hills we had to track along the many wind-ings of the river, which frequently brought the wind ahead. The entrance to the *Kien-*

teh valley, about a mile and a half in width, bore indications of having been inundated several feet deep during summer, but it was now sown with winter wheat and tur-nips, while the banks of the river were being tilled as fast as the receding water permitted. The scenery about the upper end of the river is most picturesque, and the varied foliage of the trees could scarcely be rivalled by the thousand hues which the American forests assume in autumn. The northern slopes of the mountains were clad with small firs, feathery bamboos, sundry evergreens, maples, and tallow trees, whose leaves change to the most beautiful red tints before their fall, while here and there were patches cleared amidst the dense shubbery or parched grass, carefully planted with the dark-leaved tea-plant.

As we approach the hill and mountain before us, it seems almost impossible for a river to flow from among them, but after entering the range, the small silvery streak is seen glimmering in its winding course for a long distance ahead; but at this season of the year even with unusually high water in the Yangtsze, navigation ceases at the town of *Kien-teh*, and we were told that in sum-mer few boats pass beyond the substantial bridge which spans the stream at this point, the upper navigation being full of shallows and rapids which are passed by bamboo rafts or catamarans.

But it will not do to linger over the beauty of the scenery when one's pen is in-capable of describing it, so let us proceed on our journey. It being useless to attempt to go beyond the bridge we landed on the left bank and sauntered towards the hills in search of pheasant and such small game, while our coolie was gone to enquire for a guide to take us to the mountains. We saw little on the way to the hills, which were about a mile from the river bank, and on the hill-sides the cover was too thick to expect to see anything without beaters, so we returned to the boat with a small mis-cellaneous bag of a few pheasants, a hare, and a duck or two. During our absence the coolie had succeeded in finding a genuine native sportsman, dressed in the orthodox leather 'breeks,' and the proud owner of a matchlock. He professed to know how to get at the deer and would show us where they were to be found. " Deer!—why lots of them, and many is the one I have killed, as well as wild boar," was his reply to our interrogation. This was encouraging; for to look at his odd weapon it seemed more dangerous to the possessor of it than to the foe.

It was a glorious frosty morning when we started from the boat. Our sportsman had soon found coolies to carry the baggage, and led the way through the valley to the foot of a gorge at the head of which we were to find a temple in which to pass the night. The scenery of the gorge was most striking ; and it was very pleasant to the eye, and particularly to the body to take frequent rest as we ascended the steep approach to this ancient monastery. On a sheltered knoll, about eight hundred feet above the valley, we found ensconced in a pretty little wood, the temple which was to be our shooting box for a few days. From the ascent below it was quite concealed from view by the lofty bamboos, and screened on the north by a high hill and faced on the south by a higher spur of the range of hills on which it was situated, it formed a cosy habitation for these devotees of Buddha. An old priest approaching four score years, received us in a most hospitable manner, although he had never gazed on a westerner before, and offered us the best accommodation his sanctuary would afford. It was rough in the extreme, but we considered ourselves lucky in finding a habitation of any kind in the centre of our proposed hunting ground. An unhinged door, or a few planks laid across a couple of benches served as beds, and placing these in a small ceiling-less and floorless chamber we could at least boast of a sleeping room. We dined in the presence of the gods and idols arranged in

awful array on the altar, the old priest in the meantime chanting his evening orisons, which were concluded at night and preceded at daylight by a long roll of a big drum, followed by a tolling of a large sonorous bell.

We reached the temple early in the afternoon, and not being fatigued by our forenoon walk we shouldered our guns and sauntered about in the neighbourhood of our dwelling. A herdsman whom we had met on the way up the gorge, told us that he had seen deer that day close to his cattle, with whom, according to his account, the outcast bucks appear to be fond of chumming, so we started off in search of one of these disconsolate stags. We had scarcely gone a quarter of a mile behind the wood when our "sport" cried out, " See ! see ! there they go," and sure enough there was a small herd of hinds, with a fine buck at their head, scampering off on our right, and making for the top of the hill at the back of the temple. We were so taken by surprise that it was for some time before we descried them, as, to the unaccustomed eye, they are by no means easy to see when stealing through the long grass which in autumn is much the same colour as their coats. We fired, contrary to our "sport's" advice, who, however, was not aware of the range of foreign weapons ; but it would have been better to have followed his counsel as we did not drop one, and probably lost good shots afterwards by having scared them. We got sight of the herds once more at very long range, but did not succeed in stopping any of them. Sunset was now fast approaching so we decided to return, and devise plans for the morrow's operations, but after our short experience gained by climbing to the tops of the ridges, we saw at once that in such a country it was not going to be easy work to get at them. First, the cover was so long and thick that even when out browsing they would be difficult to see ; and whether they were stalked from above or below they would be almost certain to get wind of one; then again the cover was so thick and brittle and the earth so gritty that the moment one left the deer runs or pig tracks, the noise made by the rustling of the brushwood in forcing one's way through it was quite enough to give them the alarm several hundred yards off. The stillness of the air in these hills, on a bright day, struck us as remarkable; even the movements of a little animal in the jungle were plainly heard, also the voices of the people far down the valley. The following day we proposed to get up a drive; but the beaters could not be got to work in any kind of order, so we relinquished that idea, and simply walked cautiously along the deer runs, in the hope of finding some browsing in the ravines and sunny slopes at which we might get a shot before they became aware of our approach. We were successful in seeing game, but at such long ranges that we failed to hit, or at least to bag any, although some started as if wounded, but unless hit in a vital spot they will carry away a deal of lead, and conceal themselves in the dense coppices. We continued walking along the ridge of the hill, which now became very stiff, and was leading us to the apex of the highest peak in the range. Frequent rests were willingly availed of, both to get wind and scan the valleys and ravines, for the ascent was truly as sheer as a railway cutting. While taking our ease we could distinctly hear the rustling made by a fawn pushing its way through the long grass down the hill, but it was too far to fire at, could we have drawn a bead on such a small object, which we were nevertheless anxious to procure to complete the species for our friend the naturalist.

As we were toiling up the last bit of the hill toward the summit, we spied a doe cantering round the side of a peak not far off, and thinking she might stop when out of sight of the enemy as most animals do, one of us went in pursuit; but she was lost to view, so the best thing to do was to take it easy and survey the glorious landscape,

from our elevated position—close upon 2,000 feet—for the sun was now well up towards the meridian and getting warm. The top of the hill bore signs of the recent visits of wild boars, it being rooted up in all directions. But look, what are those dirty grey animals wending their way up the hill-side from yon plantation? Pigs undoubtedly; evidently a family of them, returning from their nocturnal ravages in some unfortunate villager's garden down in the valley; and if we know their habits they will come pretty near the top of the mountain before they lie off for a bask in the genial sun. Being on the top of the hill the only thing to be done was to lie concealed and wait for their approach; but they came so slowly, as the yearlings kept gamboling about, whilst the hoary old patriarch and his lady made sundry digressions from their path to turn up some dainty root or to get a mouthful of tempting acorns or wild chesnuts. Impatient at their slow ascent, it seemed as well to sneak down through the cover toward them, as there was danger that they might take a 'doze half-way up, when a good shot might be lost. After creeping down through the cover as far as was prudent as it made such a rustling, it was disappointing to find that when we stooped down it was so thick that we could see little or nothing. The cover soon began to crackle below our position and ere long the grunting of the herd became audible, and presently the bristles of a great old boar were visible above the scrub. It was annoying not to be able to get a clear view of the heart, but it was not considered advisable he should see his enemy, for they have the reputation of charging at intruders—though our own experience proves them to be as timid as deers, if allowed room to escape—so a shot was fired at where his shoulder was supposed to be, at about 30 yards off. A thud was heard, but not a grunt or squeal did he utter, and hit in the heart the grizzly brute expired without a groan. The report of the gun naturally startled the herd, but as they saw no one they soon became quieted and commenced rooting in the covers. The absence of fear at the report of firearms when the shooter is invisible has been noticed more than once, as we shall have occasion to record. In the hurry to load up again, an S. S. G. cartridge was put into the gun instead of a ball, with the result that when it lodged in the side of a fine young porker near by, there was a prolonged squeal and struggle until it succumbed. The herd now began rushing about in dismay, some of them showing a pair of very ugly jaws as they made off into the jungle ; a charge of S. S. G. was sent after the little fry as they scampered away but without effect, nor did my companion, whom they passed at long range, manage to drop any of them. The last one hit was nowhere to be found on going to the spot where he fell, but on tracking the blood he was discovered quite dead in a thicket of grass into which he had crawled. The shot brought up the coolies, who collared the pigs and dragged them up the hill. It was a tremendous task, as they weighed several hundred weights, and until turning to get back up the hill, it did not seem that we had gone so far to "interview" the pigs. Although late in November, the noon-day sun was very warm, and after the exertion of climbing up to the summit, one felt quite prepared for a rest and some luncheon.

From the summit a fine view was obtainable of the whole country. The northern sides of the mountains were generally steep and craggy, while the southern aspect sloped down gradually to the valleys. The pasturage on the south side appeared much better, and small timber more abundant. It looked a perfect paradise for deer, and from the many runs by which the hill were traversed one would judge that they were numerous, but we received no confirmation of their numbers. Small patches of tea were seen growing at elevations of about 1000 feet, and in many places whole hillsides were planted with this shrub, the dis-

trict of *Kien-teh* being famous for its fine tea. Neither cattle nor deer appear to feed on the leaf, as it is left quite unprotected by fences, &c. Deer walks were found crossing plantations, but we could not discover that the bushes had ever been nibbled.

After an enjoyable rest we started to descend along the ridge of another spur of the range, which would lead as by a roundabout way towards our temple. We had not gone far when we halted to look at a little altar built on the top of one of the peaks. While pausing to chat and wonder what could possess the priests to build a shrine in such an inaccessible place—for it would be penance to any but a mountaineer to get up there—our attention was called to a strange noise coming below us in the gorge. It was some time before we could discover from whence it came, but on gazing far down the hill, behold, there stood an "antlered monarch of the waste," sending us a defiant cry of wonderment—

" Like crested leader proud and high,
Tossed his beamed frontlets to the sky :
A moment gazed adown the dale,
A moment sniffed the tainted gale."

We had evidently disturbed him and his beautiful hinds during their noonday slumbers, and surprised at so strange an intrusion, he sent forth that curious but derisive-like 'belling.' My companion, who was armed with a finely-sighted rifle, gave him a shot at a very long range as he went tearing down the vale, but failed to stop him. So far we had not been favored with a really good shot ; and in this country it would be difficult to stalk them if opportunity offered. Then again shooting down hill or across gorges several hundred yards wide appeared to upset the calculation of the most expert target shots, to judge from the grievous misses made. To follow deer in this curious country would be next to impossible ; for, as was remarked above, a deviation from the pig or deer walks would immediately warn the game of one's approach by the unavoidable rustling of the cover. The hills too, are so strangely formed and disconnected that to get from one range to another is a formidable undertaking.

The long tramp we had down the ridge of the hill brought no more game in view, and after a scramble through some dense jungle to take a short-cut home, we reached the foot of the gorge, when we had to commence another ascent to our temple. Climbing ever so small a hill after a hard day's march —from daylight to sunset—is a tedious operation, and it was no small relief to us when we reached the sanctuary of our hospitable old anchorite. After a hearty meal eaten while the venerable priest was reciting his evening supplications, followed by a bell and drum accompaniment, we retired to our rude couches to enjoy a well-earned repose. At cock-crow the devout old priest was up and stirring, and roused all slumberers with a long and strong roll of the big drum, and with the daylight he was chanting his morning orisons. There was no sleeping after such a thorough awakening, so we turned out to prepare for another day's sport. The adventures for the day may be briefly recounted : we worked hard, got few shots and brought nothing home. Disappointed but not discouraged, we decided to leave for the valley, and to pay another visit to this country when colder weather might make the deer less wild. After a snow-fall was the time to get them, according to our "sport," but experience has since proved that he was wrong or we ourselves very unlucky. Our return to the Yangtsze was uneventful; the geese were as unget-at-able as ever and as impervious to shot as previously, though we punted oloar up to them. Passing some fine pheasant ground we got a few brace, but being anxious to continue our explorations we had no time to make digressions into "likely" country.

The weather had been so bright and calm during our absence, and the slight breezes experienced being westerly, we were not surprised, if disappointed, to find our yacht had not turned up, but being now inured

to the discomfort of our native boat we took advantage of the fine weather and tracked from the mouth of the *Kien-teh* river to a creek at *Heang-kow* which drains lake *Tai-pih*, and which it was our intention to explore. We found the day exceedingly warm as we trudged along the river bank, gun in hand, to pick up any stray pheasants or drowsy hog-deer that might be about. A luminous and quivering haze hung about the mountains, which clearly indicated a change in this unseasonably warm weather. Our native shipper advised us not to go far up the lake as he foretold a great change at full-moon. *Pu-sa*, his idol, had acquainted him of this fact, and if we once got into the lake, and the strong northeast winds were to follow as he predicted, we should never get out until it ceased. It seemed inadvisable to go across in the face of the prophecy of this weather-wise sailor, but the country looked so inviting that my companion overruled the counsel, and across we went much to the disquiet of the skipper. We gained the southern shore before sunset and shot till it was dusk. Several pheasants fell to our guns, and to our delight an unwary goose, who came sailing over a high bluff and dropped to a charge of No. 5, after they had withstood our fusilade of small bullets. This achievement was made the excuse for a bottle of Veuve Cliquot, which we found most refreshing after the heat of the day. We started betimes the next morning intending to ascend some of the nearest hills in search of large game. But the scene was changed, and *Pu-sa's* prophecy was soon to be verified. The hilltops were capped with drifting mist ; a chill wind was blowing, and every feathered thing appeared to have sought shelter before the gale came on. We were soon driven back by rain, and scarely had we gained the shelter of our boat than it changed to snow, a sudden and trying change after the warmth of the previous days. Fully convinced in the accuracy of *Pu-sa's* prediction that we were in for a three days' gale, we did our best to endeavour to get out of the lake before the full force of it came on, but our skipper refused to stir in such a gale, as he declared we should come to certain grief. A little distance off we saw quite a fleet of staunch-looking fishing-boats beating to windward against the freshening breeze. If they could beat out why could we not do the same ? but as they tacked towards our shore we found that they were craft of a different size and build to our little shell. They were admirably handled and plunged into the snow-crested waves of the troubled lake in a manner which so excited our admiration, that forgetful of the snow, we stood watching them as we should a regatta. Probably we looked upon them as succour coming to our aid when we made out that they were bearing up for the cave in which we lay, and were hopeful that by the offer of a liberal reward they might be induced to try and make the exit of the lake. But if the tempting sight of ten Mexican dollars—the equivalent of a whole month's idleness for them—was not enough to induce them to make the attempt, it was not to be done, which proved to be the case. The wind was now blowing a perfect hurricane, so there was nothing left for us but to wrap up in our blankets, put on a cheerful countenance, and keep warmth in us by frequent draughts of Borden's condensed coffee and milk, a beverage prepared in a minute, and strongly to be recommended to all sportsmen. The storm continued the whole day with unabated fury. Towards evening our poor dogs, who, like their masters, were tired of being cooped up in so small a space, began to whine to be let loose. We gave them a run on shore, and so elated were they at their release, that they scampered away far out of hearing. Relying on the dog coolie, and on their own sagacity to come back to the boat, we paid no attention to them ; but as it was growing dusk and calling and whistling brought no response, it became evident that they must have turned up a hare or a small hog-deer (*hydnopotes inermis*)—

an animal which tempts the best-trained dogs —and given chase to it. Coolies were sent in search of them but brought no tidings.

The next day it was still blowing and snowing ; but as anything was preferable to being pent up in such a draughty boat, we agreed to brave the elements and go in search of our dogs, one of which was of great value. It was indeed hard work to make head-way on the hill tops against the blinding snow, but under the lee of hills it was endurable if not enjoyable, and the exercise had the effect of warming us thoroughly. Our search was fruitless, but during the afternoon, one of the coolies brought back the renegades, looking very penitent and hungry. They were found coiled up in a sheltered nook a long way from the boat. Late in the following afternoon the wind abated sufficiently to admit of our making for the mouth of the lake, and the following morning we found ourselves on the bosom of the muddy Yangtsze. Ere long we descried the smoke of an upward-bound steamer, and shortly after were welcomed on board by the jovial captain.

And now a few words about lake *Tai-pih* for the information of sportsmen. This lake, which it was our intention to explore, is situated at the northwest corner of the province of Kiangsi in the district of *Peng-tsih*. It empties at the village of *Hiang Kow* on the right bank of the river opposite the town of *Hwa-yang-chên*, which is distant about three miles below Dove Point. The lake extends in a south-westerly direction as far as the eye can reach, and is surrounded by high hills apparently within easy access, in which deer are said to abound. When the water in the Yangtsze is "high for the season of the year," during November, water enough will be found to get into the lake with an ordinary house-boat, but later in the season nothing but the smallest boat could get up the very circuitous creek which leads to it. A good centre-board boat would be the best to explore the lakes, as one would then be able to beat against

adverse wind when encountered. To the
sportsman who gauges his pleasure by the
number of head of game, the country in the
vicinity will not offer such attractions as
the flats about Shanghai, but to the lover
of grand scenery and noble game, the hills
of Anhui and Kiangsi cannot be surpassed.

We found the people very independent
but civil; the coolies are exorbitant in their
charges and will seldom take less than they
ask. The *Kien-têh* district had the reputation of being very anti-proselyte, but we
saw no evidence of unfriendliness. It is,
however, always advisable to avoid towns.

In another paper we hope to give an
account of some good sport.

CHINESE DENTISTRY.

[The subjoined paper is the joint production of J. G. Kerr, M.D., and G. O. Rogers,
D.D.S., embodying the observations of both gentlemen as taken on the spot, drawn up first by
Dr. Kerr and then interspersed with observations as to details from Dr. Rogers' own pen.—
ED. *China Review*.]

The practice of Dentistry in China is
doubtless very ancient, but it has not attained to the perfection which characterizes
the modern art as practised in the West.
It is, however, supposed that the Chinese
operator is possessed of superior skill in
certain points, to which his Western brother
has not been able to attain.

Inspired with zeal for an increase of
knowledge, and desiring to perfect ourselves
in the art of relieving human suffering, and
repairing the defects of human teeth, we
proceeded, on the 9th of March, 1876, to the
Temple of Horrors (Shing Wong Miu) in
Canton, where Chinese dentists do congre-
gate. We had in our minds three points
which we wished to investigate,—

1st.—The cure of tooth-ache by taking
out worms.

2nd.—Painless extraction of teeth.

3rd.—Insertion of artificial teeth.

I.—It is well known that the Chinese at-
tribute toothache to the gnawing of worms,
and that their dentists take these worms
from decayed teeth. Western physicians are
disposed to believe that there is a little jug-
glery about it, having never been able to
detect worms in the cavities of teeth. But
how the dentists performed the trick (if it
was one) and so artfully concealed it in the
hurry of daily business was a secret, and to
discover this was one object on which we
on this occasion had our purpose fixed.
We met with a rather intelligent looking
member of the profession, from whom we
obtained a lot of artificial teeth, and Dr.
R. desired to obtain a complete kit of the
tools used. In order to avoid the crowd we
invited him to a restaurant, where over a
social cup of tea, the matter was, with some
difficulty, arranged. On the following morning the man made his appearance with the
coveted implements, bringing also a lot of the
worms, and proceeded to instruct us how to
use them. His instructions or explanations
were in full accord, as far as we were able
to see, with our personal observations, as
we remained for a considerable time to
examine and study their practical operations,
several patients being treated in our presence. When a patient with toothache
applies for relief, if the tooth is solid in
the socket, the gum is separated from the
tooth with sharp instruments, and made
to bleed. During this operation the cheek
is held to one side by a bamboo spatula both

ends of which are alike and on the end held in the hand some worms are concealed under thin paper pasted to the spatula, the paper being the same color as the spatula. When all is prepared, this end is adroitly turned and put into the mouth, and the paper, becoming moistened, is very easily torn with the sharp instrument used for cutting the gums, gives up its worms, which mix with the bloody saliva, and the dentist leisurely picks them out with a pair of forceps. The patient, having ocular demonstration that the cause of his disease has been removed, has good reason to expect relief, which in most cases would be the result from the bleeding of the gum, and the fright of the patient.

When the toothache returns, as it will in almost every case, perhaps within an hour, or, may be, not for one or two days, the patient again seeks his dentist for relief, and the same operation is performed, finding more worms, which of course explains the recurring trouble, and this is continued from time to time until the tooth ceases aching altogether of its own accord from the natural death of the pulp. These worms are manufactured in quantities to suit the trade, and they are very cleverly done, yet to fully carry out the delusion the dentist is obliged to keep on hand a few live worms to show his patients, explaining that most of the worms taken from the tooth are killed either by a powder they often apply to the tooth, (it may be said that there is no virtue in the powder used) or by the process of taking them from the tooth with the forceps. Another fact might be mentioned, the standard Medical books of China teach and have taught for ages the idea of worms in a tooth causing it to ache. The above practice is resorted to when the tooth is firmly set in the jaw or is not so loose as to be removed with the finger or by a slight force or pressure with iron instruments which will shortly be described. This, our friend informed us, was an imposition, for he assured us that they could not extract teeth that were solid in the jaw.

II.—The painless extraction of teeth is accomplished by the application of a powder to the gum, which is said to loosen the tooth so that it may then be removed, after a little time, with the thumb and forefinger. The powder is useless and applied only to deceive the patient. This corresponds with what we had long known, viz. that unless a tooth had already become very loose the Chinese have no means of removing it. They do use a pair of forceps with flat jaws, but they must conceal them in a cloth because the patients are taught that no instruments are used in removing a tooth, and they are of no use unless the tooth has become quite loose. Our friend had another instrument which was merely a flat piece of iron with a hole in one end of it, the use of which was to hook on the canine teeth when they were irregular and by a sudden jerk upwards remove them. We saw a tooth removed in this way, but the instrument was concealed, and it was done so cleverly that we could not find out at the time how it was accomplished.

In the above-mentioned case the dentist applied a powder to the gums quite freely, at three different times, at each occasion letting it remain from five to ten minutes. We watched the case very closely, and concluded from the dentist's movements that he was about to extract the tooth; so while he was looking for his instruments and a cloth to conceal the same, we took the liberty to open the patient's mouth and closely examine the tooth and gum, and as was expected found the tooth and gum positively unaffected; this powder was used for no other purpose but to deceive the patient and those observing the operation. In using the thumb and fore-finger or either of the above instruments in twisting or pushing the tooth from its attachment to the gum the tooth sometimes falls upon the floor of the mouth and the patient spits it out at once, but more frequently it is left slightly attached to the gum; the tooth is then readily freed from its attachment by an almost unconscious or instinctive push or jerk of the tongue and at the same time the tooth drops from the mouth ; sometimes, however, when the tooth is not so loosened as to drop or be pushed out by the tongue, a little folded or twisted bit of paper is used, one end of which is so adjusted in the mouth that when the patient closes his teeth, which he is instructed to do, the loose tooth strikes or bites upon it, the operator then gives the paper a quick pull and out falls the tooth.*

In the removing of this canine tooth the dentist after applying the powder to his entire satisfaction, returned with a small piece of cloth in which was concealed the flat iron instrument with a hole in one end, as described above; this he kept in his right hand and in his left he had a piece of paper folded over a bit of some kind of wax, pressed flat. This wax is called toothache plaster, and has in it some supposed charm or power to help loosen the tooth. After the powder had done its work, the dentist then struck the patient several slight blows in quick succession upon the cheek just behind the region of the tooth to be removed with this charmed toothache plaster ; this was done to divert the attention of the patient for the moment while at the same time, with his right hand he appeared to be rubbing the gum with this cloth, but in fact was adjusting the instrument upon the tooth ; then with a very quick jerk upward and outward he dragged the tooth in part from its socket (the patient wincing considerably): this upward jerk was so quickly and adroitly done that it would be quite liable to deceive a close observer, having the appearance at most of an accidental catch on the tooth or perhaps a hasty movement of the hand from the

patient's mouth up over his head as the operator stepped hurriedly back to his traps which were lying behind the patient, as though he was in quest of another toothache plaster, which in fact was the case, and on his return he went through the same operation as before, and out came the tooth.

There are many kinds of powders used by different dentists, but as our friend confessed, they are all a sham. The recipe for the one he uses is as follows :

馬螂螂 Ma-long-héung.
川烏 Ch'ün-û.
草烏 Ts'ò-û.
生半夏 Shang-pún-há.
白芷 Pák-chi.
川芎 Ch'ün-kung.
土狗 T'ò-kau.
白芍 Pák-chéuk.

III.—The insertion of artificial teeth has been practised in China for ages before it was introduced into Europe, and has one great recommendation, viz. cheapness. In this respect our Western dentists cannot rival the operators of the Flowery Kingdom. The material used is bone or ivory, and the tooth having been sawn and filed into the proper shape, is fastened to the adjoining teeth by a copper wire or cat-gut string. If two or more teeth are required, they are made in one piece and a hole drilled the whole length, through which a double string or wire is passed, which loops over the natural tooth at one end and is tied to the tooth at the other. This work, although rude in the extreme, is as to looks better than the absence of the teeth, and is of some use in mastication.

The cost of a single tooth will be from 5 to 10 cents, and the charge for half a dozen would be from 30 cents to half a dollar. At these low rates all classes may avail themselves of the benefit, and those who practise the art do a thriving business.

---

* I have several kinds of Chinese powder for loosening teeth and have applied it to the gums according to instruction and found in each case that it did not affect the gum or loosen the tooth in the least. We never have made a chemical analysis of either of these powders.
                                G. O. ROGERS.

CHINESE INTERCOURSE WITH THE COUNTRIES OF CENTRAL AND WESTERN ASIA DURING THE FIFTEENTH CENTURY.

PART II.

A Chinese Itinerary of the Ming period from the Chinese North-western frontier to the Mediterranean Sea.

(Continued from page 182).

When I promised, in the introduction to my paper, to give a translation of this ancient document, I had estimated its value only after a cursory inspection; and had been struck particularly by the great amount of Geographical details it seemed to bring forward in sketching the overland route from China to Western Asia. But after I had set myself about to examine it critically I found that the Chinese text is full of inaccuracies, which render its Geographical value very problematical. However, notwithstanding these frequent errors, which have crept in particularly with respect to the distances and directions noticed,[*] it cannot be denied, that the above-named itinerary contains a nucleus of authentic information ; the greater part of names of places met in it are easily recognized as Turkish or Persian names, and evidence for the real existence of such names may probably be found in the ancient Persian Geographical dictionaries. Thus there is no room for the surmise that the whole itinerary should have been forged in China. But it may be, that it has been taken down from the accounts furnished by

[*] We read almost always west instead of north-west and south-west.

Chinese travellers from memory after their return to China. A great number of the inaccuracies in the Chinese text are due evidently to clerical errors, as I shall prove in comparing two copies of the text in my possession. I am far from claiming a high importance for these fragments of ancient Asiatic Geography, but I consider them sufficiently interesting to be rescued from oblivion, all the more as they bear on the great mediæval lines of travel through Central Asia. I must confess however that I am often puzzled what to make of the places enumerated in that ancient itinerary, and our knowledge of the tracts, which come here into consideration, is still so defective, that, being apprehensive of misleading the reader, I generally abstain from venturing any conjectures.

The Chinese itinerary, of which I attempt here to give an English version, bears the title 西域土地人物畧 *Si-yü-t'u-ti-jen-wu-lio*, *i.e.* sketch of the countries, the people and the products of the *Si-yü*, and thus professes to be a descriptive account of the regions in the west. But it will be seen that these notices bear rather the character of a road book, for the information occasionally introduced with respect to the enumerated places is very scanty and seldom contains anything characteristic, whilst the distances between the cities and stations and the direction of the road are generally noticed.

The *Si-yü-t'u-ti-jen-wu-lio* has been preserved in the 天下郡國利病書 *T'ien-hia-kün-kuo-li-ping-shu*, which is a strategical description of China, published from 1639 to 1662. Thus the publication began at the close of the Ming period. The author of the ancient itinerary, which is found in Chap. CXVII of the afore-mentioned work, is not named there, and we are also without explanation as to its origin. But in all probability the information, dealt with in it, dates from the 15th century, when Chinese envoys visited Western Asia almost every year, and the commercial intercourse between China and the countries in the west was also very animated. It may be, that it has been compiled in China from various itineraries, and this would explain the confusion which has crept into the statements.

The Chinese text of the itinerary, as it appears in the *T'ien-hia-kün-kuo* etc., gives in large characters only the names of the cities and stages on the main roads and the respective distances, whilst the notes added are printed in small characters and present some meagre descriptive accounts with respect to these places, and frequently mention also places situated out of the great highway.[*]

Some of the names of places met in the Chinese itinerary are Chinese names, *i.e.* the Chinese characters representing these names express a meaning and may give in some cases a translation of the corresponding Turkish or Persian names. But generally the foreign names of places are simply rendered by similar Chinese sounds.

I owe to the kindness of Archimandrite

[*] In my translation I shall follow the same order as in the Chinese text and put the notes in small type.

Palladius another copy of the *Si-yü-t'u-te-jen-wu-lio*, which has been copied out, I am not prepared to say, from what work of the Imperial Chinese library. When compared with the text found in the *T'ien-hia-kün-kuo* this manuscript copy shows some differences in the spelling of the names as well as with respect to the estimation of the distances. I translate the text of the *T'ien-hia-kün-kuo* etc., but shall point out the divergences of the manuscript text.[*]

The Chinese itinerary to the countries in the west begins at *Kia-yü-kuan*, the important defile at the north-western frontier of China, (compare *China Review*, Vol. IV., p. 313, a, Note †). Although the greater part of the Geographical names mentioned on the route and in the vicinity of it escape critical investigations—owing to the scantiness of our knowledge with respect to these tracts from other sources ancient or modern — we are nevertheless enabled to trace in a general way the lines of the itinerary. The mentioning of such places as *Sha-chou*, *Ha-mi*, *Kharakhodja*, *Turphan*, *Kucha*, *Aksu*, *Kashgar* in the first part of it, leaves no doubt, that it follows the great highway through Eastern Turkestan along the southern slope of the *T'ien-shan* chain. As we have learned from the accounts translated in the first part of this paper from the Ming-shi, this was indeed the way by which the numerous embassies from the various countries of Western Asia used to proceed to China. Even the embassies from Badakhshan seem to have preferred this route to the shorter way passing by Khotan and Lopnor, on account probably of the great deserts the traveller has to cross in the latter direction. This fact is confirmed also by the narratives of Shah Rukh's embassy to China (1420), and Hadji Mahommed's account of Cathay (1550). Goës (beginning of 17th century) passed also through Aksu, Turphan, Hami, when proceeding to China. In the days of

[*] The abbreviation M.S. relates to the manuscript copy of the itinerary.

Mongol supremacy however, in the 13th century down to the reign of Kublai khan (1260), the great line of comunication between eastern and western Asia lay along the northern slope of the T'ien-shan (Karakorum, Urumtsi, Kuldja, Chu river, Talas, Sairam, Samarkand). Karakorum was at that time the residence of the Mongol Khans, and this way was indeed the shortest from the Mongol capital to Transoxiana. (See my *Notes on Chinese Mediæval Travellers*).

After Kashgar we meet in our itinerary a series of names of places for which I have not been able to trace any corroboration elsewhere, and then five names appear, which are easily recognized as those of five cities of Farghana, viz: *Andidjan*, *Sharikhana*, *Marghilan*, *Ush*, and *Kanibadam*. From Farghana we are led to Herat, but before reaching this city the itinerary notices a number of names of places situated north and south of the road or on it, amongst which we recognize the city of *Kaluga*, coupled with the *Iron Gate* and the cities of *Kunduz*, *Khulm*, *Balkh*, and *Andhui*. After Herat we have *Merv*, *Bokhara*, *Samarkand* and many other names unknown to me.

The rest of the itinerary is very dark and confused. Among the numerous Geographical names appearing in it I can trace with more or less certainty only the following places: *Badakhshan*, *Bastam*, *Astrabad*, *Shiraz*, *Isphahan*, *Sultanieh* (?), *Tabris* (?), and four months' journey west of the latter *Constantinople*. Hence we are transported to *Bagdad* and then led to *Mecca*, *Medina*, *Egypt*. From Egypt the itinerary turns to Asia Minor, at least among the cities mentioned further on we can recognize *Sivas*, *Atina*, *Angora*, *Kutahieh*, *Brussa*. After Brussa the sea (Mediterranean) is noticed with big men of war navigating in it. The last city spoken of in the itinerary is *Lu-mi*, 1400 *li* west of Brussa. It seems that *Rome* is meant.

The Chinese author who is responsible for the present sketch of the road to Western Asia has generally rendered with great correctness by Chinese sounds the foreign names of the places he notices in Central and Western Asia, but he was frequently mistaken with respect to the distances and the direction. He seems to have been under the impression that the whole route he traces in the itinerary follows a direction straight to the west. As I have shown in the afore-sketched summary the route line followed in it is quite irregular. The inaccuracies with respect to the estimation of distances may partly be explained by clerical errors.

After these introductory remarks let us now turn to the translation of the *Si-yü-t'u-ti-jen-wu-lio*, which I shall try to render as literally as possible, even with all its descriptive vaguenesses.

Proceeding west from 嘉峪關 *Kia-yü-kuan** (defile of the delicious valley) 80 *li* one arrives at 大草灘 *Ta-ts'ao-t'an* (marsh of high grass)

This country is vast and rich in grass.

40 *li* west of the marsh is 回回墓 *Hui-hui-mu* (Mohammedan tombs).

There are three great sepulchral mounds. Hence the name. Out of the way, to the north, is the monastery of 鉢和寺 *Po-ho-sze*, and 50 *li* west of this monastery is the town of 紫城兒 *T'ze-ch'eng-r* (purple town).†

20 *li* west of the Mohammedan tombs is the city of 騸馬 *Shen-ma* (geldings city).

In the city there are three brooks flowing to the north.

3 *li* (30 *li* M.S.) west of *Shen-ma* is 三顆樹 *San-k'o-shu* (the three trees).

There are three (remarkable) trees. Hence the name.

---

* In the narrative of B. Goës' itinerary (beginning of the 17th century) it is termed Chiaicuan (Yule's *Cathay*, p. 579.)

† The terms 城 ch'eng and 城兒 ch'eng-r (diminutive of ch'eng) occur frequently in the text of the itinerary. I translate the first always by "city" the second by "town." Likewise I translate 山 shan by "mountain" and 山兒 shan-r by "hill."

30 *li* (M.S. 50 *li*) west of the three trees is the city of 赤 斤 *Ch'i-gin*. *

A military post has been established here in the beginning of the Ming. Out of the way 20 *li* southward is 小 赤 斤 *Siao Ch'i-gin* (little *Ch'i-gin*).

50 *li* west of *Ch'i-gin* is the city of *K'u-yü* (bitter or distressed valley). †

The Ming established here a military post. East of *K'u-yü* is 河 城 *Ho-ch'eng* (river city) and in it are 3 (2 M.S.) mounds (墩). 50 *li* to the north is 王 子 莊 *Wang-tze-chuang* (cottage of the little prince).

20 *li* west of *K'u-yü* is 古 墩 子 *Ku-tun-tze* (old mound), ‡ and west of this mound is a tower (塔).

60 *li* west of the old mound is the city of 阿 丹 *A-dan*.

To the north-west is a river and north of

* The Ming History (see above beginning of the article Ch'i-gin and Note ‡, page 34) gives also an itinerary from Kia-yü-kuan to Ch'i-gin. The names of the stations enumerated here are about the same as named in the present itinerary, but there are great divergencies in the two accounts with respect to the distances. According to the Si-yü-tu-ti etc., Ch'i-gin is 173 *li* distant from Kia-yü-kuan, whilst the Ming-shi estimates the same distance at 240 *li*. In a modern Chinese register of distances, referring to the post roads in eastern Turkestan, the following figures are given :—

From Kia-yü-kuan to 雙 井 子 Shuang-tsing-tze (double well) 40 *li*—further to 回 回 堡 Hui-hui-p'u (Mohammedan fort) 50—to the lake Ch'i-gin 70. Thus from Kia-yü-kuan to lake Ch'i-gin 160 *li*. Further on 40 *li* is the 赤 斤 峽 Ch'i-gin-hia (defile of Ch'i-gin). These places are also marked on the great Chinese map.

† The city of K'u-yü is repeatedly mentioned in the Ming-shi (see above articles Hami and Sha-chou and Note *, page 22, a). The Ming-shi states that K'u-yü lies 200 *li* west of Ch'i-gin. On the great Chinese map K'u-yü is marked about 100 *li* west of the city of 玉 門 Yü-men. According to this map the ruote to Hami now-a-days does not pass through K'u-yü, but leads from Yü-men in a north-westerly dircetion to the city of An-si, etc.

‡ Tun, a mound, means also a distance mark, and here in the ancient itinerary this character is probably to be taken in this sense.

the river is 羽 郎 戎 卜 隆 吉 兒 *Yü-dsi-jung Ba-lung-gi-r*. *

30 *li* south west of *A-dan* is the city of 哈 喇 兀 速 *Ha-la-wu-su* (*Khara-ussu* = Black water (river) in Mongol).

North-west of *Ha-la-wu-su* is the city of 义 班 *I-ban* and between the two cities is a river.

100 *li* south-west of *Ha-la-wu-su* is the city of 瓜 州 *Kua-chou* † and 60 *li* further west is the city of 西 阿 丹 *Si-A-dan* (western *A-dan*).

50 *li* south-west of the afore-mentioned *I-ban* is the city of 卜 隆 吉 兒 *Bu-lu-ng-gi-r* and 80 *li* south-west of this place the roads unite in western *A-dan*.

On the southern road are the following places : 垣 力 *Yüan-li* 提 乾 卜 剌 察 提 兒 卜 剌 額 吉 也 大 羽 大 温 *T'i gan bu la ch'a t'i r bu la gi me da yü da wen* (evidently these characters represent several names).

On the northern route are 襖 赤 瞻 永 *Ao-ch'i-djan-yung*, 恒 力 *Heng-li* (垣 力 *Yüan-li* M.S.) 哈 剌 哈 剌 灰 *Ha-la-ha-la-hui*.

West of the city of western *A-dan* are 兀 兀 兒 禿 *Wu-wu-r-t'u* 牙 兒 小 剌 陳 *Ya-r-siao-la-ch'en* (*Ya-r-bu-la-ch'en* M.S.), 荅 失 卜 剌 *T'a-shi-bu-la*, and north of western *A-dan* : 王 子 莊 樹 *Wang-tze-chuang-shu* (the tree of the cottage of the little prince),—north-west of western *A-dan* : 哈 剌 灰 *Ha-la-hui* 台 温 虎 都 乩 失 虎 都 *T'ai-wen-hu-du-kia-shi-hu-du* 俄 偏 肖 *Wo-p'ien-siao*, 阿 赤 *A-ch'i* 卜 兒 邦 *Bu-r-bang* (*Bu-r-na* M.S.), 哈 卜 兒 葛 *Ha-bu-r-go*, 賽 罕 *Sai-han*.

* The great Chinese map marks a place and a river of this name on the road from Kia-yü-kuan to Hami. The river has to be crossed near An-si.

† Kua-chou is marked on the great Chinese map south-west of the city of An-si. Now-a-days the road to Hami does not pass through Kua-chou. The Ming-shi, art. Sha-chou, states that Kua-chou is 190 *li* south-west of K'u-yü.

200 *li* (100 M.S.) west of western *A-dan* is the city of 沙州 *Sha-chou*. *

The Ming established a military post at *Sha-chou*. In ancient times the country here was called 流沙 *Liu-sha* (see *China Review*, Vol. IV, p. 313 b, Note *). West of *Sha-chou* are the cities of 虎木哥 *Hu-mu-k'o*, 答失虎都 *Da-shi-hu-du*, (*Bu-ya-la* M.S.), 牙卜剌 *Ya-bu-la* 哈失卜剌 *Ha-shi-bu-la*. North-west (of *Sha-chou*) are 阿子罕 *A-dze-han*, 阿赤 *A-ch'i*, 司尹克 *Sze-i-k'o* (引只克 *Yin-dji-k'o* M.S.), 哈密頭墩 *Ha-mi-t'ou-tun* (this could be translated : first distance mark on the territory of Hami), 羽木脫云 *Yü-mu-t'o-yün*, 乞兒把赤 *K'i-r-ba-ch'i*, 克兒革也思 *K'o-r-go-ye-sze* (克兒乜草思 *K'o-r-me* (lie) *ts'ao-sze* M.S.)

300 *li* west (it should be north-west) of *Sha-chou* is the city of 哈密 *Ha-mi*. †

East of the city is a river with a bridge over it. There is also a water-mill. 30 *li* north of *Ha-mi* 速卜哈剌灰 *Su-bu-ha-la-hui*,‡ 30 *li* south is 畏兀兒把力 *Wei-wu-r-ba-li* (Uigurbalik.)

10 *li* west of *Ha-mi* is the city of 阿思打納 *A-sze-da-na*.§

* Concerning *Sha-chou* compare Note * page 120, b and the respective article on this place translated in this paper. There it is stated, that *Sha-chou* is situated 440 *li* (an erroneous figure) west of *Kua-chou*. The Ming Geography however (art. Ch'i-gin) reckons 180 *li* only from Ch'i-gin to the frontier of *Sha-chou*.

† Thus according to the Si-yü-t'u-ti etc. from Kia-yü-kuan to Hami 1020 *li*, whilst according to the Ming History this distance is 1600 *li*. In modern Chinese itineraries it is estimated at 1470 *li*. Judging from our maps the distance between the afore-mentioned places, as the crow flies, may be about 1,000 *li*.

‡ This is probably the same as the 素木哈兒灰 *Su-mu-ha-r-hui* mentioned in the Si-yu-wen-kien-lu (I. fol. 4) among the six cities subject (in the last century) to the prince of Hami.

§ A-sze-ta-ni is mentioned in the Si-yu-wen-kien-lu (l. c.) as one of the six cities subject to the prince of Hami.

50 *li* (M.S. 10 *li*) north of *A-sze-da-na* is 卜吉兒 *Bu-gi-r* and 50 *li* west of *Bu-gi-r* is the city of 阿打納 *A-da-na*. Further to the west is 也帖木兒 *Ye-t'ie-mu-r* (也帖木兒 *Me-t'ie-mu-r* M.S.) Further westward 50 *li* is the city of 剌木 *La-mu*. Further to the west are 把兒海子 *Ba-r-hai-tze* (*Ba-r* lake),* 雙山兒 *Shuang-shan-r* (double hill), the mountain 嶮把兒 *Hien-ba-r*, the 雙山兒 *Shuang-shan-r* (double hill), the city of 鉢和寺 *Po-ho-sze*. 50 *li* (10 *li* M.S.) west of this city is 哈剌帖 乩 *Ha-la-t'ie-kia* and from this place north-west 10 *li* (50 M.S.) is the city of 剌木 *La-mu*. West of *Ha-la-t'ie-kia* is 察克兒 *Ch'a-hei-r*. There is also a river † and in it is the city of 霙家 *Shuang-kia* (double family,—the M.S. has 霙泉 *Shuang-ts'üan* double spring). 100 *li* west is 雙泉兒墩 *Shuang-ts'üan-r-tun* (mound of the double spring.)

West of *A-sze-da-na* is 把兒思潤 *Ba-r-sze-k'uo*. Further westward is the town of 脫合 *T'o-ho*.‡ Further to the west is 比昌 *Pi-ch'ang*. § Further west is the city of 魯珍 *Lu-djen*.||

* Perhaps lake Barkul is meant, for "kul" means lake in Turkish.

† 川 Chuan means generally river, but sometimes a plain is designated by this character.

‡ T'o-ho is probably the city of 托和蘑 T'o-ho-ts'i on the great Chinese map, marked there north-west of Hami. In Captain Trotter's itinerary from Turphan to Hami (Survey Operations in Eastern Turkestan, 1873-74, p. 159) it is termed Taghochi.

§ This is the 闢展 P'i-chan of the great Chinese map, between Hami and Turphan. In the narrative of Goës' travels a city Pucian is mentioned, but west of Turphan, Col. Yule (Cathay etc. p. 578) supposes that P'i-chan is meant but that the diarist has transposed the name. See further on Note * page 232, b.

|| In the Ming History (see above) this place is styled Liu-ch'eng or Lu-ch'en. On the great Chinese map the name reads 魯克沁 Lu-k'o-ts'in. Capt. Trotter (l.c.) writes Lukchun. Ac-

South of the city are 剌士 *La-t'u,* 蘆菱芋墩 *Lu-ling-yü-tun* (mound of rushes, caltrops and taro. The M.S. has 蘆葦艸墩 *Lu-wei-ts'ao-tun,* mound of rushes and grass), the city of 懶眞 *Lan-djen,* the mound of 半截土 *Pan-tsie-t'u* (cut in two), the mountain of 巴思濶 *Ba-sze-k'uo.*

North of *Lu-djen* is the city of 羊黑 *Yang-hei,** and 50 *li* further west is 哈剌火者 *Ha-la-huo-djo* '(Karakhodja).† Further west 50 *li* is the city of 我答剌 *Wo-da-la.* Further west 100 *li* is 土魯番 *T'u lu fan* (Turphan.)‡

The 囘囘 *Hui-hui* (Mohammedans) there till the ground and cultivate many fruits and trees. To the north is 委魯母 *Wei-lu-mu.* §

200 *li* west of *T'u-lu-fan* is the city of 俺石 *An-shi.*

South of *An-shi* is the town of 俺鼻 *An bi,* to the north is the tank (lake) of 撒剌 *Sa-la.*

Further west 50 *li* is 蘇巴失 *Su-ba-shi* ‖ (蘇巴赤 *Su-ba-ch'i,* M.S.)

To the north is the town of 兔眞 *Mien-djen* (兔眞 *T'u-djen,* M.S.)

Further west 200 *li* is 昆迷失 *Kun-mi-shi.*¶

cording to Klaproth (Mém. rel. à l'Asie, II. 342) the city is called also Lukchak by the Mohammedan writers.

* Yang-hei may be the place Yanghi-khhin in Capt. Trotter's itinerary, between Lukchun and Karakhodja.

† ‡ With respect to Karakhodja and Turphan see above the respective articles translated from the Ming-shi.

§ Perhaps Urumtsi is meant.

‖ Su-ba-shi is also found on the great Chinese map on the road from Turphan to Karashar. It appears also in Trotter's itinerary (l.c. p. 158) between the same cities.

¶ On the great Chinese map we find a place 庫木什阿哈瑪 *K'u-mu-shi A-ha-ma* marked between Sa-ba-shi and Karashar. In Capt. Trotter's itinerary the name reads Kumush

South of it is the *white hill* and from this hill the city of *An-bi* (see above), to the east, can be reached in six days. North (of *Kun-mi-shi* or perhaps of the white hill) is a tank (lake) and the town of 昌都剌 *Ch'ang-du-la.*

200 *li* west of *Kun-mi-shi* is 阿剌木 *A-la-mu** and further west 100 *li* is the city of 乂力失 *Yu-li-shi* 乂力失 *I-li-shi* M.S.)

South of this city is the river 俺林 *T'u-lin.*†

100 *li* west of *Yu-li-shi* is the city of 哈剌哈失鐵 *Ha-la-ha-shi-t'ie.*‡

(ibid. p. 158). Trotter adds, that the road passes through hills.

* I am disposed to identify this place with the Aramuth in Goës' itinerary (Yule's Cathay, p. 578) although it is located there between Turphan and Khamul. But as in the same itinerary Pichan is erroneously mentioned west of Turphan (see Note ‖, page 231), it may be that Pichan and Aramuth have been mutually transposed by the diarist. A place Aramut appears also in the relation of Timur's expedition against the Jetes, in 1379 (see Note *, page 109 above). Petis de la Croix identifies it (Hist. d. Timur-Bec), quite arbitrarily, with Karakhodja.

† Perhaps the river Tarim is meant, which according to the Chinese maps empties itself into the Lopnor.

‡ It seems that by this name Karashar is intended. The character *t'ie* may be a misprint. If my identification be right, this would be the first instance of the name of Karashar appearing in Chinese works. I have not been able to trace it in any of the Chinese works of the Mongol period. It is also not mentioned by the \ ohammedan writers of the 13th and 14th centuries. Even Goës in the beginning of the 17th century when passing from Kuch'a to Turphan does not notice a place of this name. It seems to me, that among Western Travellers Mir Izzet Ullah (1812-18) is the first who had heard of the city of Karashar, situated on the road to China, between Kuche and Turphan (Yule's Cathay, p. 576.) To the Chinese the city of 哈剌沙兒 *Ha-la-sha-r,* as they now spell the name, became more generally known in about the middle of the last century, when Emperor K'ienlung's armies made the conquest of Eastern Turkestan and Dsongaria. In modern Chinese Geographical works Harashar is identified with ancient 焉耆 *Yen-ki,* first mentioned in the History of the former Han in the 2nd century B.C. as a realm in the Si yü, situated in the vicinity of a lake, abounding in fish. By this lake, according to the Chinese, the Bostangnor is meant. Yen-ki is spoken of in the Chinese

South of it are the town of 卜 *Bu* (格
卜 *Go-bu* M.S.), and the city (river M.S.)
of 扯 力 昌 *Ch'e-li-ch'ang** ; to the north
are the town of 苦 他 巴 *K'u-t'a-ba* †
and the river of 黑 松 林 *Hei-sung-lin*
(black pines forest).

100 *li* further west is the spring of 瀼
巴 *Jang-ba*, and 100 *li* further west is the
黑 水 泉 *Hei-shui-ts'uan* (black water
spring.)‡

North of this spring are : the city of
察 力 失 *Ch'a-li-shi*,§ the town of 丁
Ding, the 泉 兒 河 *Ts'üan-r-ho*.

annals down to the 10th century. In the days
of the T'ang it was a Chinese military district.
On the great Chinese map Karashar is placed a
little north-west of lake Bostang and north of
the river 開 都 *K'ai-du*, whilst south of the
river 古 城 *Ku-ch'eng* (old city) is marked.
The Chinese state (Father Hyacinth's Dsungaria
and Eastern Turkestan, p. xxxviii) that the present city of Karashar has been recently built (*i.e.*
in the last century) but that the ruins of two
ancient cities can be seen there. Karashar is
placed on our maps after the astronomical de-
terminations made in 1760 by order of K'ienlung by the Jesuit missionaries d'Arocha, Es-
pinha, Hallerstein (Ritter's Asien, I, 324.) As
far as I know no European has since that time
visited this city. Karashar means "black city."
* Archimandrite Palladius has identified this
place with the Charchan of Marco Polo. See
Journal of N. Ch. Br. Asiat. Soc. for 1876, p. 2.
† A place 古 塔 巴 *Gu-t'a-ba* is marked
on the Chinese Mediæval map upon which I
commented in my Notices of Mediæ. Geogr.,
see page 189. I believe it to be the same as
Khutukbai on modern maps situated on the
route from Urumtsi to the Kuldja. There is
also a river of this name, which takes its rise
north-east of Karashar.
‡ There is on the great Chinese map the
name of a place 哈 刺 不 刺 *Ha-la-bu*
(*Karabulak*=black spring) marked not far from
庫 兒 勒 *K'u-r-le* (Korla) on the road from
Karashar to Kucha.
§ This is probably the city of Jalish mentioned
by Sherif-eddin as a place, where Timur passed,
on his way to Yulduz (which, as is known, is
situated to the north-west of Karashar.) See
above Note *, page 109. According to Hadji
Mohammed's itinerary (circa 1550) Cialis lies
midway between Kucha and Turfan (10 days'
journey to either of these places. See Yule's
Cathay, p. 576.) In Goës' itinerary (l.c. p. 574)
Cialis is noticed as a small place 25 days (travel-
ling slowly evidently) east of Cucia (Kuchar.)

(Spring river). To the south is the city of
扯 力 昌 *Ch'e-li-ch'ang*.*

100 *li* west of *Hei-shui-ts'üan* is the city
of 雙 山 兒 *Shuang-shan-r* (double hill),
and further west 100 *li* the town of 獨 樹
Tu-shu (solitary tree).

North of this town are the rivers 兀 馬
Wu-ma and 撒 力 瀼 巴 *Su-li-jang-
ba*, to the west is the 一 晝 夜 川 *I-
chou-ye-ch'uan* (river, or perhaps plain, of
one day and one night).

100 *li* west of *Tu-shu* is the well of 察
力 察 *Ch'a-li-ch'a*.

North of the well is the 火 炎 山 *Huo-
yen-shan* (fire mountain).†

Further west 200 *li* is the 淤 泥 泉
Yü-ni-ts'üan (muddy spring).

South of the spring is the town of
克 列 牙 *K'o-lie-ya*. From this town
eastward to the city of 扯 力 昌 *Ch'e-
li-ch'ang* (see above) are 8 stations.

100 *li* west of *Yü-ni-ts'üan* is the river of
察 兀 的 *Ch'a-wu-di*.

Mountains adjoin this river from the
south and the north.

100 *li* west of this river is the river of
楊 子 *T'a-tze*.

* This name occurs for the second time in the
itinerary. I am not aware whether that same
place is meant as mentioned above south of Ha-
lu-shi-t'ie.
† Probably some volcanoes in the T'ien-shan
chain are alluded to. Chinese Geographers
state, that "burning caverns" are found in the
mountain range of the T'ien-shan, on the whole
distance from Turphan to Kucha (Arch. Palladius, l.c. p. 2.) The Si-yü-wen-kien-lu, in
describing the burning caverns north of Kucha
states, that in them spontaneous fire can be seen
in spring, summer and autumn. The fire becomes extinct in winter time owing to snowfalls
and the great cold. Then the people of the
country enter naked these caverns to gather
硇 砂 *nao-sha* (Sal ammoniac.) Capt. Trotter
(l.c. p. 147) reports, on the authority of a Pundit
attached to the mission and who visited Kucha,
that according to the people there a sort of rat
circulates freely in the flames (of the caverns)
without being injured and that it goes by the
name of Salamander. Compare also M. Polo's
account of the salamander.

It is also bordered by mountains from the south and the north.

10 li west of the river T'a-tze is the city of 古克兀 Gu-k'o-wu.

North of it lies the city of 雅思雅阿 Ya-sze-ya-a. To the south is the 潦池 Lao-ch'i (puddle tank.)

Further on 100 li is the city of 苦先 K'u-sien,* and 100 li further west the city of 西牙河 Si-ya-ho (river Si-ya.)†

North of this city are: the 雙山關 Shuang-shan-k'an (defile between two mountains), the city of 阿思馬力 A-sze-ma-li. To the north-west is the lake of 迤西澗 I-sze-k'ao.‡ To the west is 沙的郎哈 Sha-di-lang-ha, to the south-west the river of 花提 Hua-di, to the south 赤刺店 Ch'i-la-tien (the inn of Ch'i-la).

300 li west of Si-ya-ho is the city of 阿黑馬力 A-hei-ma-li, and further on 100 li south-west is the city of 土力苦扯 T'u-li-k'u-ch'e (Li-t'u-k'u-ch'e M.S.)

From this place the city of 擺 Bai§ in the east is distant 40 li.

100 li north-west of T'u-li-k'u-ch'e is the city of 阿速 A-su (阿迷 A-mi M.S.)‖

* K'u-sien is probably the Cucia of Goës (Yule, l.c. 573) and the 庫車 K'u-ch'e of modern Chinese maps. On our maps the name is styled Kuche, Kucha (Russian maps), Kuchar (Capt. Trotter, l.c. p. 147.) Compare also Note * page 109 and Note ‖ page 181 above, and my Notices of Mediæv. Geogr., etc. p. 149.

† According to the Si-yü-wen-kien lu there is 60 li south-west of K'u-ch'e a Mohammedan city 沙雅兒 Sha-ya-r. Capt. Trotter (l.c. p. 116) notices a river of this name near Sairam.

‡ Evidently lake Issikul, see Note * page 116, a, is meant.

§ This is the same as the city of 拜 Bai on modern Chinese maps. Now-a-days the great highway from Kucha to Aksu passes through Sairam and Bai. The Ming itinerary leads us by a more southern way from Kucha to Aksu.

‖ This is the city of Aksu in Eastern Turkestan. Aksu means white water or river. The statement in our itinerary about the three cities adjoining each other is corroborated by Sherif eddin, who, in relating Mirza Eskender's

There are 3 cities adjoining each other and surrounded by mountains and rivers.

200 li west of A-su is the city of 阿赤地里 A-ch'i-di-li (阿亦城里 A-i-ch'ng-li M.S.)

North of this city is the river 也列 Ye-lie, * to the south is the city of 阿丹 A-dan, to the west is a spring.

Further west 100 li is the city of 克力賓 K'o-li-bin. †

South of it are two (remarkable) Mohammedan tombs and the 黑玉河 Hei-yu-ho (river of black jade.)‡ To the north is the 石店子 Shi-tien-tze (stone inn.)

expedition against the Jetes in 1399, states, that the latter captured Aksu, a very strong place, consisting of three forts communicating with each other (see Note * page 109.) Aksu appears also in Hadji Mohammed's itinerary (circa 1550, Yule l.c. ccxvii.) Goes' way to China led also through Aksu (l.c. 571.) In the middle of the last century the Jesuit missionaries determined Aksu astronomically (Ritter's Asien, I. p. 324.) The information about Aksu and the way thither, as communicated in Capt. Trotter's report (l.c. 144,) has been given by a Pundit attached to Sir Douglas Forsyth's mission. It seems that the name Aksu was unknown before the Ming period. At least I have not been able to trace it earlier either in Mohammedan or in Chinese works. I therefore think, that Deguignes' view, that Aksu is identical with the Auxacia of Ptolemy, has no foundation and is as much arbitrary as the identification of modern Chinese Geographers, who suggest, that Aksu is the same as the country of 溫宿 Wen-su, described as a realm of the Si-yü as early as in the second century B.C. Now-a-days the Chinese spell the name of Aksu 阿克蘇 A-k'o-su.

* Perhaps the river Ili is meant, which lies indeed north of the regions here spoken of.

† Sherif eddin mentions a place Kelapin on the road from Yarkand to Aksu (see above Note * page 109). Capt. Trotter states (l.c. p. 26) that Kalpin is situated between Ush Turpan and Maralbashi, about 15 tash (67 Eng. miles) distant from the latter place, which is about midway between Yarkand and Aksu.

As we shall see further on, our itinerary leads to Kashgar, and as a name like Ush does not appear in it, it can be assumed that it follows a more direct way to Kashgar, passing south of Ush.

‡ The Karakash river, or river of black jade, is west of Khotan (see above Note † page 118, a). But here in the itinerary perhaps the Yarkand river is meant. The Si-yü-wen-kien lu (II. fol. 15) states, that jade is obtained also from the latter.

Further west 100 *li* is the 乾泉 *Kan-ts'üan* (dried-up spring), and again 100 *li* west is a great well (大井).

South of the well is the 三築城 *San-chu-ch'eng*[*] (city three times raised.)

200 *li* west of the great well is the inn of 比長 *Pi-ch'ang*.[†]

South of it is the town of 乾羊 *Gan-yang*. To the north is 石城兒 *Shi-ch'eng-r* (stone town.)

200 *li* further west is the 土臺泉 *T'u-t'ai-ts'üan* (spring of the earthen terrace.)

On this terrace there are two springs. Hence the name. South of it is the city of 拾本干 *Shi-ben-gan* (恰木石干 *K'ia-mu-shi-gan* M.S.)

200 *li* west of the springs is the river 桐 *T'ung*.

South of it is the city of 牙力干 *Ya-li-gan*[‡] (于力于 *Yü-li-yü* M.S.), and to the north is 石城 *Shi-ch'eng* (stone city.)

50 *li* further west is 石子泉 *Shi-tze-ts'üan* (stone spring).

West of the spring is 把力站 *Ba-li-djan* (station of *Ba-li*). To the south is 店子井 *Tien-tze-tsing* (well of the inn), to the north is the town of 養泥 *Yang-ni*. This town is distant from *Shi-ch'eng*, situated to the east (see above), 8 stations.

100 (200 M.S.) *li* west of the stone spring is the city of 河西丁 *Ho-si-ding*.

South of the city is the town of 瑣河 *So-ho* (river *So*), and to the south-east is a lake.

* In the Si-yu-wen-kien-lu (II. fol. 14) a city 三珠 San-chu is mentioned among the cities depending on Yarkand.
† Pichan, more than 100 miles distant from Kashgar, on the road connecting the latter city with Ush Turphan (Trotter l.c. 25). On the great Chinese map this place is styled 闢展 P'i-djan.
‡ Yarkand.

200 *li* north of *Ho-si-ding* is the city of 亦的哈馬 *I-di-ha-ma*. South-west of it is the city of 哈失哈力 *Ha-shi-ha-li*,[*] and 50 *li* west is the city of 失哈力 *Shi-ha-li*.

South of this city is the city of 米兒阿都剌 *Mi-r-a-du-la*. To the west are: a river, and (a place) 民運 *Min-yün*. To the south are: 也民運力灰 *Ye-min-yün-li-hui* (也力灰 *Ye-li-hui*, M.S.), 黑沙納思 *Hei-sha-na-sze*, 哈北民運 *Ha-bei-min-yün* (哈劄 *Ha-dja* M.S.) To the north is the city of 黑失哈 *Hei-shi-ha* (黑決哈 *Hei-küe-ha* M.S.)

Further west is 尚力 *Shang-li* (南力 *Nan-li* M.S.), and further west 300 *li* is 我撒剌 *Wo-sa-la*.

South-west of this place is 計墩巴失 *Gi-dun-ba-shi* (討墩巴失 *T'ao-dun-ba-shi* M.S.) To the north-west is the city of 賽蘭 *Sai-lan*.

Further west 500 *li* is the city of 土剌 *T'u-la*.

This city is of a roundish form with houses round about. A little prince is ruling there. The Mohammedans (in that country) do not wear turbans but caps made of sheep's wool. They do not till the ground. They eat fish, mutton and mare's milk.

Further west 700 *li* is the city of 牙思 *Ya-sze*.

The Mohammedans there wear turbans. Among the products of the country are mentioned: 凌羊角 *ling-yang-küo* (antelope horns, see Note * page 25,a) 帖角皮 *t'ie-küo-p'i*.[†]

400 *li* west of *Ya-sze* is 也失卜 *Ye-shi-bu*.

* Kashgar. Compare my Notices of Mediæv. Geography etc., p. 153.
† Compare above, end of the article Lu-mi.

South of this place are 巴速兒 *Ba-su-r*, 打卜你俺的速 *Da-bu-ni-an-di-su*. To the north is the city of 他失干 *T'a-shi-gan*.

300 *li* west of *Ye-shi-bu* is 亦爾乞咱打班 *I-r-k'i-dsa-da-ban.*

South of it are: 大熱水泉 *Ta-jo-shui-ts'üan* (the great hot spring), 黑水泉 *Hei-shui-ts'üan* (black water spring), 亦可速巴 *I-k'o-su-ba*. To the north are: 黑石城 *Hei-shi-ch'eng* (black stone city) and the city of 賽蘭 *Sai-lan*.

Further west 200 *li* is 亦乞咱打班 *I-k'i-dsa-da-ban*, and further west is the city of 把力干 *Ba-li-gan*.

South of this city are 哈剌界 *Ha-la-kiai*, 阿必打納思乞亦咱撒剌思咱力沙亦乞咱力 *A-bi-da-na-sze-k'i-i-dsa-sa-la-sze-dsa-li-sha-i-k'i-dsa-li* (Evidently several names of places. I do not know how to divide. Instead of the first two characters *A-bi* we read *Ha-mi* in the M.S.).

500 *li* west is the city of 俺的干 *An-di-gan.†*

North of this city is 馬兒黑納 *Ma-r-hei-na.‡*

Further west 700 *li* is the city of 我失 *Wo-shi.§*

South of it are 懶澗 *Lai-kien* (rivulet *Lui*), 馬答剌撒 *Ma-da-la-sa*, 大者阿力 *Da-djo-a-li* (火 | | | *Huo-djo-a-li*, M.S.). To the east is 郎弩古力 *Lang-nu-gu-li*.

* Daban means "defile."
† Andidjan in Farghana.
‡ Probably Marghinan (Marghilau) in Farghana. This place is however south-west of Andidjan.
§ Ush in Farghana.

Further west 300 *li* is the city of 馬都 *Ma-du*.

Seven water branches have been conducted to this city, where they unite. To the south there is a high mountain, to the north is 沙兒黑納 *Sha-r-hei-na.**

50 *li* south-west of *Ma-du* is 砍的把丹 *K'an-di-ba-dan†* (炊 | | | *Ch'ui-di-ba-dan* M.S.).

West of this place are 咱力都 *Dsa-li-du*, 罕都 *Han-du*, 撒力赤剌牙 *Sa-li-ch'i-la-ya*.

300 *li* north of *K'an-di-ba-dan* is 黑寫歪 *Hei-sie-wai*.

North-west of this place is the city of 虎帖 *Hu-t'ie*, and 400 *li* west of it is 阿若懶 *A-jo-lai* (阿懶答 *A-lai-da* M.S.).

Further west 300 *li* is 阿力砍打思 *A-li-k'an-da-sze* (| | 炊 | | *A-li-ch'ui-da-sze* M.S.)

South of it are : 兀魯兩尊 *Wu-lu-liang-dsun* 阿拜郎力姐民 *A-bai-lang-li-dsie-min* (| | 卽 | | | *A-bai-dsi-li-dsie-min*, M.S.), 兩六七 *Lang-liu-ts'i* (| | 乜 *Liang-liu-me* M.S.) There is a water mill. 300 *li* north-west is 阿懶答 *A-lai-da*, and north-west of the latter is 阿迷脫 *A-mi-t'o* (| 速 | *A-su-t'o* M.S.)

Further west is the city of 亦卜剌 *I-bu-la*.

The city is surrounded by water from four sides. (The country) produces sugar. South of *I-bu-la* are 答黑答弇 *Da-hei-da-ben*, 的火著 *Di-huo-djo*, 昆都思 *Kun-du-sze,‡* 剌巴的木耳咱亦卜剌 *La-ba-di-mu-r-dsa-i-bu-la*, 哈兒

* Sharikhana lies between Andidjan and Marghinan.
† Kanibadam, south-west of Kokan.
‡ Kunduz, south of the Amudaria.

斤 *Ha-r-gin*, 哈沙打 *Ha-sha-da*, the city of 戶倫 *Hu-lun*,* 速兒哈 *Su-r-ha*† (達 | | *Da-r-ha* M.S.) 聆黑的 *Hi-hei-di* (貯 | | *Dju-hei-di* M.S.). North of *I-bu-la* are 鐵門關‡ *T'ie-men-kuan* (Iron gate), the city of 克力干 *K'o-li-gan*§ (| | 于 *K'o-li-yu* M.S.) the cities of 把黑里 *Ba-hei-li*,‖ 失巴力 *Shi-ba-li*, and 俺的灰 *An-di-hui*.¶

Further west is the city of 黑樓 *Hei-lou*.**

In this country *lions* are found and 哈剌若术 *ha-la-jo-shu* (| | 苦 | *ha-la-k'u-shu* M.S.).*** It produces also western horses, gold, silver, precious stones, silkstuffs, different kinds of cotton, fruits, etc. The people till the ground.

South of *Hei-lou* 400 *li* is the town of 赤鐵旦黑猪黑答蘭 *Ch'i-t'ie-dan-hei-dju-hei-da-lan* (Instead of the second character *t'ie* the M.S. has 戲 *hi*). There are further, south of *Hei-lou*, the cities of 巴巴沙忍 *Ba-ba-sha-hu* and 剌巴留剌阿力阿 *La-ba-liu-la-a-li-a* (| | | 的 | 阿 | *La-ba-di-la-*

* Khulum, west of Kunduz.
† Surkhab is another name for the Wakhsh, a tributary of the Amudarin.
‡ The Iron-gate. Compare above Note ‡ page 130.
§ Kaluga is another name for the Iron-gate (see Note † page 130). Perhaps the K'o-ligan in the itinerary refers to the town, which according to the Mohammedan authors stood at the Iron-gate.
‖ The second and the third characters have evidently been transposed. Then Ba-li-hei would denote Balkh.
¶ Audkhui, west of Balkh.
** It seems, that by Hei-lou, Heri or Herat is intended. In the Ming History Herat is termed 哈烈 *Ha-lie* or 黑魯 *Hei-lu*, but there is also an article devoted to the country of 黑樓 Hei-lou, the king of which by name of Sha-ha-lu (Shah-Rukh) had sent tribute to China. (See above my translation of these articles). It seems to me that the compilers of the Ming History have made some confusion and owing to the different spellings of the names took Hei-lou and Halie or Hei-lu for distinct countries.
*** Karagush or Siah-gush (black-eared) is the Persian name for the hunting lynx, Felis Caracal. See also Note † page 126, b.

ho-li M.S.). North-east of *Hei-lou* is the city of 馬力 *Ma-li*.*

Further to the west is the city of 阿倫 *A-lun*.

East of *A-lun* is 失黑山河 *Shi-hei-shan-ho* (This could be translated mountain and river of *Shi-hei*).

Further west is the city of 火者阿都阿剌墨蠻 *Huo-djo-a-du-a-la-hei-man*.

South of the city is the mountain of 失黑 *Shi-hei*. To the north-west is the city of 剌八的 *La-ba-di*.

Further west is 阿力伯 *A-li-bo*.

The *hui-hui* (Mohammedans) there wear turbans. South of *A-li-bo* are 阿剌都伯 *A-la-du-bo*, 黑失 *Shi-hei*, 阿力店子 *A-li-t'ien-tze* (the inn of *A-li*).

West of *A-li-bo* is the city of 禁民 *Dsa-min*.

South of this city is 阿思民 *A-sze-min*.

500 *li* (50 *li* M.S.) west of *Dsa-min* is the city of 普合 *P'u-ha*.†

The people of the country are Mohammedans. They till the ground, cultivate sundry fruits and breed silkworms. *P'u-ha* is subject to *Sa-ma-r-han*. South of *P'u-ha* is 剌巴子火馬黑麻撒力瓦思 *La ba dze huo ma hei ma sa li wa sze* (these 11 characters represent probably several names). To the north are 卜剌撒瓦剌思 *Bu-la-sa-wa-la-sze* and the city of 克力干 *K'o-li-gan* (| | | 于 *K'o-li-yu* M.S.)

500 *li* west is the city of 楷馬兒罕 *Sa-ma-r-han*.‡

* There is probably a character wanting in this name. It seems to me that Mern or Mero is intended. The historians of the Mongol period styled Mero Ma-li-wu. See Notes of Mediæval Geography etc., p. 198.
† Bukhara.
‡ Samarkand.

The people there are Mohammedans and wear turbans. They breed silkworms, cultivate sundry fruits, fine grapes, cotton etc. They have mules of large size. The country produces also precious stones, gold, silver, fine steel 魚牙把力 *yü-ya-ba-li*,[*] 帖角皮 *Tie-kio-p'i*.[†] Lions and 哈剌苦术 *ha-la-k'u-sha*[‡] are met in that country.

To the north of *Sa-ma-r-han* is the city of 阿力 *A-li* and a 望日樓 *wang-ji-lou* (tower for observing the sun,—an observatory).

500 *li* west is the city of 失剌思 *Shi-la-sze*.[§]

The people there are Mohammedans. They wear turbans and till the ground.

Further west 300 *li* is a high mountain.

To the south are mountains. To the north is 馬土力 *Ma-tu-li*, to the north-west is the town of 撒子 *Sa-dze* and further north-west is 巴黑打帖 *Ba-hei-da-t'ie*.

Further west is the city of 把答山 *Ba-da-shan*.[‖]

青金石 *ts'ing-kin-shi* (Lapis lazuli) is found there. South of *Ba-da-shan* is the city of 西河 *Si-ho*; north of Badashan is 阿沙巴力 *A-sha-ba-li*.

1500 *li* west is the city of 怯迷 *K'ie-mi*.

It is ruled by a little prince, outside the city are four foreign and Chinese families living (四族番漢). The country produces gold and diamonds. South of *K'ie-mi* are: 牙兒打兒 *Ya-r-da-r* and 阿巴的納都 *A-ba-di-na-du*.

Further west is the city of 新旦 *Sin-dan*.

The Mohammedans there wear turbans and till the ground. The country produces rice, millet and sundry fruits. South of *Sin-dan* are the cities of 巴答力山 *Ba-da-li-shan* and 阿力伯 *A-li-bo*.

400 *li* west is the city of 孛思旦 *Bu-sze-dan*.[*]

The Mohammedans there till the ground, breed silkworms, etc. To the south of *Bu-sze-dan* are the Mohammedan cities of 阿力阿伯 *A-li-a-bo* and 俺的灰 *An-di-hui* and the town of 黑著沙平 *Hei-djo-sha-p'ing*.

500 *li* west of *Bu-sze-dan* is the city of 亦思他剌八 *I-sze-t'a-la-ba*.[†]

It is a Mohammedan city. The country produces rice, millet; the people till the ground and breed silkworms. South of *I-sze-t'a-la-ba* is the city of 盼的干 *Hi-di-gan* (盼的干 *P'an-di-gan* M.S.) Lions and 哈剌 *ha-la*[‡] are found there. There are further the cities of 巴巴沙葱 *Ba-ba-sha-ts'ung*, 戶倫 *Hu-lun*, 剌巴的咱兒答 *La-ba-di-dsa-r-da*, 剌巴的迷 *La-ba-di-mi*, 剌巴的打爾斤 *La-ba-di-da-r-gin* (*La-ba-di-ba-r-gin* M.S.)

600 *li* west of *I-sze-t'a-la-ba* is the city of 失剌思 *Shi-la-sze*.[§]

The Mohammedans there wear turbans. The country produces *yü-ya-ba-li* (see Note [*] page 238, a) sundry fruits, etc. There is 長流水 *Ch'ang-liu-shui* (long flowing river.)

Five days' journey west is the Mohammedan city of 亦思 *I-sze*,[‖] which is subject to *T'ie-kia-lie-sze* (see further on).

---

[*] A product unknown to me. Yü-ya means fish teeth. Compare also above article T'ien-fang. It was stated there, that in 1518 the Prince of Mecca sent as present knives made of fish teeth.
[†] See end of article Lu-mi, above.
[‡] See Note *** page 237.
[§] Sherakhs. See Note * page 170, a.
[‖] Badakhshan.

[*] Bostham, south-east of Astarabad.
[†] Astarabad.
[‡] See Note *** page 237.
[§] Shiraz.
[‖] Probably two characters are missing. In the Ming-shi Isphahan is rendered by 亦思弗罕 *I-sze-fa-han*.

The country produces 阿魏 *a wei* (*Asa-fatida*, see Note * page 25, b) 阿芙蓉 *a fu jang* (Opium.) The people manufacture woollen stuffs, satin, variegated carpets, 𪨊幅 *so fu* (see notes * 123, a, and * 169, b.) To the south are the cities of 阿巴的納都打剌木角 *A-ba-di-na-du-da-la-mu-kio*, 馬失卜 *Ma-shi-bu*, 剌巴的扯帖兒統都兒 *La-ba-di-ch'e-t'ie-r-t'ung-du-r* (instead of *t'ung*, the M.S. has *jang*) 剌巴的米納牙 *La-ba-di-mi-na-ya*. To the north-west is a great plain (大川, which means also great river.) It takes 10 days to cross it.

Further west 800 *li* is the city of 瑣力旦 *So-li-dan*.*

The Mohammedans there wear turbans, and till the ground. There are 黑狐 *hei-hu* (black foxes) in that country. To the south is the city of 若鸞 *Ju-lan* (苦蘭 *K'u-lan* M.S.), to the north the city of 亦的 *I-di*.

West of *So-li-dan* is the city of 阿郎民 *A-dsi-min*.

It is ruled by a little prince subject to *T'ie-kia-lie-sze*, (see further on.) The country produces *a-wei* (Asa-fœtida.)

Further west is the city of 帖亢列思 *T'ie kia lie sze*.†

It is ruled by a little prince. The people manufacture variegated carpets. To the east 6 days' journey is the city of 阿力旦 *A li dan*, To the south-east is the town of 瑣力 *So-li* (頗力 *P'o-li* M.S.) To the north-east is the city of 紐扎 *Niu-dja*.‡

* Perhaps Sultanieh between Kazwin and Zendjan. See my Notices of Mediæv. Geography, p. 206.

† The second character 亢 *Kia* may probably be a misprint for *Po* 白. Then the name would read *T'ie-bo-lie-sze* and might mean Tebris.

‡ Nakhidjevan?

Further to the west, 4 months' journey, is the city of 苦思旦 *K'u-sze-dan*.*

It is a Mohammedan city. The people wear turbans. To the south-east is 也兒的 *Ye-r-di*.

Further west is the city of 沙密 *Sha-mi*.

It is also a Mohammedan city. The country produces several kinds of fruits, fine grapes. There is a breed of horses called 哈剌骨 *Ha-la-gu*.†

One month's journey further west is the city of 把黑旦 *Ba-hei-dan*.‡

Seven water branches have been conducted to this city, where they unite. 2000 Mohammedan families live in it. Lions, *ha-la k'u-shu* (see above note ***** page 237), and leopards are found in that country. To the south the city of 欠土 *K'ien-t'u*, to the north is the city of 陝西斤 *Shan-si-gin*.

Further west is the city of 也的納 *Ye-di-na*.§

It is a Mohammedan city. The people wear turbans.

Further west 100 *li* is 飯店兒 *Fan-tien-r* (hostelry) and further west, six day's journey, is the kingdom of 天方 *T'ien-fang*.‖

The (principal) city is surrounded by two walls, Mohammedans are living in it. Other Mohammedan people arrive at T'ien-fang from other countries to pray there. To the south is the well of 架子 *Kia tze*. To the north is the city of 阿思納 *A-sze-na*.

* It seems to me that Constantinople is meant. To the Arabs, Persians and Turks this city was known in the middle ages under the name of Constantinah. It is styled Ki-sze-dan-i on a Chinese Mediæval Map. See my Notices of Mediæv. Geogr. etc., p. 221.

† See Note * page 125, b.

‡ Bagdad.

§ The first character 也 *Ye* in this name seems to be a misprint for 乜 *Me*, and then the name of the city of Medina would be exactly rendered by the Chinese characters. The Ming-shi writes this name Mo-de-na. See above.

‖ Mecca. Compare above, article T'ien fang, translated from the Ming shi.

15 stations west of the kingdom of *T'ien-fang* is the city of 米饥力 *Mi-kia-le** (米的力 *Mi di-li* M.S.)

It is a Mohammedan city.

Further west is the city of 牙瞞 *Ya-men.*

There are black-haired Mohammedans. The country produces agathe, amber etc.

Further west is the city of 文谷魯 *Wen-gu-lu.*

The Chinamen living there have all dishevelled hair and wear caps. There are coral trees found and also looking-glass stones with seven kinds of flowers and herbs on them 眼鏡石上有七樣花草. East of the city is a river, which is crossed in row boats.

Further west is the city of 阿都民 *A-du-min.*

It is also a Mohammedan city.

Further west is the city of 也勒朶思 *Ye-le-do-sze.*

This city is surrounded by water which is crossed in row boats. The Chinese there have all dishevelled hair and wear caps. The country produces rice, sundry fruits etc. The people manufacture 撒黑剌 *Sa-hei-la* (see above Note † page 123) and 鑌鐵刀 *Pin-t'ie-tao* (knives made of fine steel, see Note * page 21, a).

Further west is the city of 撒四賽 *Sa-sze-sai*† (撒黑四賽 *Sa-hei-sze-sai* M.S.).

It is enclosed by three walls. All the Chinamen living there have dishevelled hair and wear caps. Sundry precious woods and medicines are found there.

Further west is the city of 哈利迷 *Ha-li-mi.*

The people there are Mohammedans, wear turbans, breed many sheep and horses, cultivate rice, yellow grapes and other fruits.

Further west is the city of 阿的納 *A-di-na.**

It is a Mohammedan city, subject to *Lu mi* (see further on.)

Further west is the city of 菲即 *Fei-dsi.*

It is surrounded by two walls and ruled by a little prince. The Chinamen there shave their hair and wear caps. Rice is cultivated. Different silkstuffs, carpets, etc. are manufactured there.

Further west is the city of 安谷魯 *An-gu-lu.*†

It is a Mohammedan city. The same products as enumerated in the afore-mentioned places. The city is situated near a mountain. On this mountain is a superintendency (山上有巡檢司.)

Further west is the city of 可臺 *K'o-t'ai.*‡

The people are Mohammedans, till the ground, cultivate cotton. At the foot of the mountains 西天紅花 *si-t'ien-hung-hua* (Saffron) is cultivated. West of the city is a river and on it are two water-mills.

Further west is the city of 孛羅撒 *Bu-lo-sa.*§

It is likewise a Mohammedan city. To the south-west (west M.S.) is the sea. In it the people navigate large ships (men of war.) They are so big, that they can load rations for 1000 men and for 3 months. These ships are also provided with weapons of war of every kind.

* I suppose, that in this name the last two characters are wrong and that originally Mi-si-r was intended, which, as we have seen, denotes Egypt.

† Perhaps Si-was, in Asia Minor, a very strong place stormed by Timur in 1400.

* There are two cities of Asia Minor to which this name could be referred, both mentioned by Sherif-eddin in connection with Timur's expedition, viz.: Atina, located on Petis-de-la Croix's map (l.c. III.) opposite Cyprus and Adin south-east of Smyrna.

† Angora in Asia Minor.

‡ Kutahieh in Asia Minor.

§ Brussa in Asia Minor.

Further west is the city of 魯迷 Lu-mi.*

* It is difficult to say where the Chinese itinerary intends to place Lu-mi. Judging from the distance from Brussa noticed, we should refer Lu-mi to Rome. However there were hardly Mohammedans in Rome. Compare also above the article Lu-mi translated from the Ming-shi.

It is situated 1200 li west of Bu-lo-sa and enclosed by two walls. It has an independent ruler. The inhabitants are Mohammedans; there are also Chinamen and interpreters.

E. BRETSCHNEIDER, M.D.

A LEGEND OF THE PEKING BELL-TOWER.

[For the subject of the following verses, I am indebted to a paper on Chinese Legends read before the North China Branch of the Royal Asiatic Society by Mr. Stent some years ago, and I feel that I owe that gentleman an apology for daring to walk in a "magic circle" which he has made so peculiarly his own.]

In Peking to the northward
　　There stands a belfry-tower,
Whence rings the warlike tocsin
　　To warn of danger's hour;
And mournful is the legend
　　The Peking people tell
Of Mandarin, and maiden,
　　And the casting of the bell.

Yung-lo* sat throned in Council
　　And thus aloud spoke he:
"I have built the town a bell-tower
　　"Both high and fair to see;
"Yet is there one thing lacking
　　("See ye advise me well);
"To whom shall be committed
　　"The casting of the bell?"

Then out spoke Chung the elder,
　　A mandarin of fame:
"There is no man in Peking
　　"More worthy we should name
"Than he who cast the cannon
　　"Which guard the city well;
"Kuan-yu† who cast the cannon
　　"Good sooth can cast the bell."

* 永樂 Yung-lo, third Emperor of the Ming Dynasty, 1403-1425.
† Kuan-yu is said to have been a mandarin of the second grade.

Yung-lo and all his Council
　　Assented with one voice,
And the vermilion pencil
　　Confirmed the Council's choice.
"Hither be Kuan-yu summoned
　　"That Our own lips may tell
"On him the lot has fallen
　　"To cast the monster bell."

And in the Council chamber
　　Before his lord Yung-lo,
Kuan-yu received the message
　　And thrice performed Kotow.
And many a night of watching,
　　And many a magic spell
Were his who had been chosen
　　To cast the monster bell.

The month of preparation
　　Has glided to its close;
The mould stands there completed,
　　The molten metal glows.
With sound of drum and cymbal
　　And brazen trumpet's swell,
With courtly crowd of high degree
The Emperor has come to see
　　The casting of the bell.

The mould is standing ready,
　　The molten metal glows;

The Emperor lifts his finger,
  The hissing metal flows.
But till the iron hardens,
  Where is the man can tell
If Fate has cursed or favoured
  The casting of the bell?

————

YUNG-LO sat throned in Council,
  And at his feet full low
KUAN-YU lay humbly prostrate
  And thrice performed *Kotow*,
" What Heaven decrees for mortals
  " In every thing is well:
" Heaven sped not with its blessing
  " The casting of the bell."

————

Then YUNG-LO answered mildly :
  " We know that men are frail,
" And how a want of forethought
  " May make their efforts fail.
" Another month we grant thee,
  " Be thine to use it well ;
" Be diligent, be careful,
  " And cast another bell."

————

The sleepless nights of watching,
  The weary days ran on ;
Once more the mould stood ready,
  The molten metal shone,
The Emperor and courtiers
  Came with the trumpet's swell ;
The hissing metal filled the mould,
  The seething mass grew hard and cold :
  Heaven grant a better bell !

————

YUNG-LO sat throned in Council,
  And wrath was on his brow ;
KUAN-YU lay humbly prostrate
  And thrice performed *Kotow*—
With trembling and with terror
  Did he the tidings tell
How Heaven had cursed in anger
  The casting of the bell.

————

Then YUNG-LO answered sternly
  To fury was he wroth :
" 'Tis thou hast played the sluggard,
  " Thine is the traitor's sloth !

" One other month we give thee ;
  " 'Fore Heaven, use it well !
" Thy head shall pay the forfeit
  " For such another bell !"

  .   .   .   .   .   .

————

Among the Peking maidens
  Ko-AI* unrivalled goes ;
Hers are the raven tresses
  And hers the cheeks of rose.
Whence are those falling tear-drops ?
  What makes that bosom swell ?
Her father's life is hanging
  On the casting of a bell.

————

With muffled face and figure
  Who steals through evening's shade
To seek the dread magician ?
  'Tis Peking's loveliest maid.
With muttered incantation,
  With mystic charm and spell
She learns why Heaven above is cold
And why the Powers of Air withhold
  Their blessing from the bell.

————

She leaves the dread magician
  And closer draws her veil ;
Her eyes dilate with horror,
  Her cheeks are ashen pale.
Well might the spirits' answer
  Sound to her like a knell :
A MAIDEN'S BLOOD MUST MINGLE
  WITH THE METAL OF THE BELL.

  .   .   .   .   .

————

Another month of watching
  Has hurried to its close ;
The Emperor gives the signal,
  The seething metal flows.
The hissing metal rushes
  Into its destined cell,
And with a wild despairing cry,
  " Father, for thee ! " the brave KO-AI
Has flashed to where the bubbles gleam,
Has cast her headlong in the stream
  And mingles with the bell !

    * Ko-ai 可 愛 i.e. the lovable.

Kʋan-yu with horror started
  To seize her as she passed ;
He caught her by the slipper
  And thought to hold her fast,
In vain ; the frantic father
  Uttered a maniac yell ;
The day that wept for fair Ko-ai,
That day saw Kuan-yu's reason die,
  And wrought a wondrous bell.

———

And while the bell is tolling
  Half by its clanging drowned

A plaintive *hsieh, hsieh,*[*]
  Follows the louder sound.
" Ko-ai asks for her slipper,"
  The listening people tell,
" Ko-ai the fair, Ko-ai the good,
" Who for her father gave her blood
  " To mingle with the bell."

G. M. H. Playfair.

[*] *Hsieh* 鞋 a shoe, or slipper. This word, pronounced in Pekinese *see-ay*, not inaptly represents the sound of a large bell " whishing " through the air.

———————

A CHINESE HORNBOOK.[*]

The Indian Barrister who wrote to the *Times* some time ago complaining that his country was called barbaric, an epithet which seemed to him, and justly, much the same as barbarous, certainly shewed himself both valiant and cunning of fence when he delivered the home thrust that, with all our civilisation, India manages, and for centuries has managed the pauper question better than we do. And he shewed himself not only cunning of fence but also possessed of tact and delicacy, when he touched very lightly indeed on such sores as our national drunkenness, and the charmingly refined manners of our operative classes, not even hinting, but only indicating almost imperceptibly how he might hint, that a nation should not be too ready to fling about hard words like *barbaric*, which has not yet succeeded in teaching its women to dress on public occasions with common decency, and which goes to the Derby.

That these rebukes, or ten thousand of them, will fall off unfelt from the thick hide of British complacency, there can be

[*] 幼學初階 by the Rev. Charles Piton. Published by the Hongkong Elementary School-books Committee.

no manner of doubt. For our cherished habit, in all questions of civilisation, is first of all to assume the whole question at issue by postulating a definition of civilisation entirely favourable to ourselves. Briefly, civilisation is whatever is English, and whatever is not foreign. This mental attitude is closely akin to that of the irrepressible 'Arry whom we meet in *Punch.* " Well, *I* think a man never looks so well as in the 'Ighland costume," says 'Arry, being at that moment in the costume in question, but not on the whole looking well in it.

Had the Prince of Wales come to China instead of going to India, it might have been necessary for a Chinese Barrister to enter his protest against the generosity in epithets manifested by the *Times* or the *Daily Telegraph.* China, perhaps, would not have got off with barbaric ; she certainly would not have received an elaborate apology from the leading Journal in the shape of a demonstration that barbaric does not mean barbarous. And yet the Chinese barrister might have pointed out that, with all our civilisation, and all our parliamentary grants, they manage, and for centuries have managed the education question better in China than we do.

Yes, we should say, you educate a larger percentage of children, as far as can be ascertained, or you educate the same percentage with infinitely less fuss. But see what an incomparably superior article we supply! Look at your poor little pagans "suckled in a creed outworn," and then at our national school children, seeing pictures of railway engines and telegraphs, and enduring object lessons on every conceivable subject.

With great deference, however, I venture to doubt whether what the average village child picks up at a national school, unless supplemented by home or fortuitous training, is so much more or so much better than what a Chinese child acquires at the hot and crowded village academy. According to a member of the London School Board † the normal child of the English working classes learns ;—

1.—To read, write, and cipher, but generally not so well as to take pleasure in reading, or to be able to write the commonest letter properly.

2.—A quantity of dogmatic theology.

3.—A few of the broadest and simplest principles of morality.

4.—A good deal of Jewish history and Syrian geography; perhaps a little something about English history and geography.

5.—A certain amount of regularity, attentive obedience, and respect for others.

Now, except the Jewish history and Syrian geography, this is very much what A-chan or A-pat gets in his three years under the village dominie. The dogmatic theology is represented by a good deal of dogmatic paganism, for the most part equally true, and certainly equally useful; whilst against the absence of the Syrian geography, or of any geography at all, we may set the fact that A-chan learns to read so as to take some amount of pleasure in reading, even if his prose composition is not exactly all it ought to be.

† Professor Huxley, *Lay Sermons*, p. 40.

On one point, however, it must be admitted that the English school has fairly an advantage. In it, unless mismanagement and inertia reign supreme, you find the children supplied with little books compiled by men who have made teaching a science, who know exactly what are the difficulties their subjects present to the average child, and who have devoted the patient labour of years to anticipating and minimising those difficulties. There is Arithmetic made easy, Grammar made almost rational, Geography made positively interesting, and History that has learned not to talk about Anglo-Saxons. Such books, in the hands of a competent teacher, are what a drop of oil is to a lock or bolt. You *can* force it home without the oil, but with what labour and pains; whereas, with the oil, how smoothly and pleasantly it goes.

Such books are, however, a very recent development of education. It is not long since we were teaching boys Latin grammar in Latin, and making them commit to memory *Propria Quae Maribus* whether they understood it or not, a very Chinese practice. *Henry's First Latin Book* is a modern invention, and I believe schools (or more probably " academies ") still exist in England where they use the crude manuals of Walkinghame, Magnall, Lindley Murray, and Pinnock, none of them a century old, hopelessly out of date as they are.

But in China, until the publication of the little work under review, it might almost have been said that even the humble *Reading made easy* had yet to be invented. There are a few books for children of course, books for boys, and books for girls, very much the Mrs. Trimmer sort of book; but when you come to teaching children to read, there is nothing specially adapted to the purpose. The only plan is to get something easy and make the child read it, as Mrs. Wesley dragged her unhappy infants neck and crop to the first chapter of Genesis. How the poor innocents must presently have tumbled over Mehujael, Methuselah, and Mahalaleel.

But even they, with some sort of conception of the meaning of what they read, had an easier task than the Chinese child, for our young friend A-chan is set down to a nice little primer of thirty pages, of which this is the first:—

昔　教　苟　性　人
孟　之　不　相　之
母　道　教　近　初

擇　貴　性　習　性
鄰　以　乃　相　本
處　專　遷　遠　善

and he is told, Read that, and learn it by heart. If any reader, unskilled in Chinese, has followed me to this point, I can put him in the same position by saying, Read that, and learn it by heart.

But, falters the unhappy pupil, feeling as if he had been told to fly, or to walk on the sea, how *am* I to read it? Well, I don't mind telling you that the first character* is *yan*, the next *chi*, and the next *ch'o*. The next three are *sing*, *pán*, *shin*, and so on throughout the page. You will please to pay attention to the exact sound of every one, so that, when I have bawled it at you some half dozen of times, you may be able to bawl it to yourself. You will then learn the page by heart, and, for a change, may trace the characters through thin paper, and so learn to write them.

But what do they mean, what is it all about? That is the very question you are not to ask. If you persist in pestering to know what it means, you will make an unpleasantly close acquaintance with a piece of rattan which lies on my desk. You must go through it, page after page, until you know the whole by heart, and can write it, and then perhaps, after a fashion, we will tell you what it means. The important point is, however, not what it means, but that when you have mastered it you will

know 573 characters.* As this number is not nearly sufficient for the business of writing and reading, you must commence another and harder book, and learn it in the same way.

The only thing in our own system of education at all comparable to this frightful drudgery is learning the alphabet—twenty-six arbitrary and meaningless signs, arranged anyhow nohow. But there are only twenty-six of them, and against their unsystematic arrangement are set such refreshing facts as that A was an archer and shot at a frog. If there were successive alphabets, each of five hundred letters or so, more anyhow nohow than ever, and unmitigated by one single allusion to Archers or Apple-pies, our little ones might reasonably complain, more than they do, of the "wearisome bitterness of their learning."

We are now in a position to appreciate the Rev. C. Piton's attempt to provide something to bring A-chan and A-pat past that wearisome bitterness a little more pleasantly, an attempt which he felicitously calls his Chinese Hornbook. Here is the first lesson :

一
二
三

The mere English reader has already guessed that these signs mean One, Two, Three, and when I tell him that they are pronounced *yat*, *i*, *sám*, he knows just as much about them as did Confucius or Mencius, and as much as Choo Hi *knew*, but not quite as much as he dreamed and fancied, which however is of consequence to no mortal. When you have got the sounds of these by heart, and have traced, and so learned to write them, and *know what they*

* Begin at the upper right hand corner and read downwards.

* The book contains 1071, but of these 498 are repetitions.

mean, there follows a reading lesson, which I reproduce in English. It is not a page to be learned by heart, it is something to be read, as we understand reading.

Lesson I.

One, two, three.—Three, two, one.—One, three.—Three, one.—One, three, two.—Two, one, three.—Two, three, one.—Two, two, one. —Three, three.

After this follow three more large characters for tracing :—

人

几

又

The teacher would proceed to explain the sounds and meanings of these as follows :— (1) *yan,* a man, men; (2) *yap,* to come in, coming in, come in, &c.; (3) *yau,* also. The reader who has followed me so far now knows six Chinese characters, and knows also, except their exact sound, which can only be caught from *viva voce* instruction, all about them that he need wish to know. The next reading lesson combines and exercises us in all we have learned.

Lesson II.

One man. Two men. Three men. Man *by* man. A man *is* coming in. *He* also *is* coming in. One man also came in. One *or* two men. Two men also came in. Two *or* three men. Three men also came in. Man *by* man *all* also came in. Two *or* three men came in.

So we go on, through fifty lessons, until at the end of the book we are reading such sentences as these :—" The east is where the sun rises. The west is where the sun sets. To pray God for rain. To beg food of people, &c., &c.," the principle kept in view being, very little new matter in each lesson, with continual repetition of what went before.

It is true that the pupil now knows only 274 characters, but how does he know them? He can read *and understand* any piece of Chinese which consists only of those 274 or

of any of them—he could write a simple letter by their aid. He is in the position of an English child who can read words of one syllable, and to this position he has been brought almost pleasantly. He has *read* his book, it has not been hammered into him, nor is he dependent on knowing it by heart, but can read it backwards, forwards, "dodging" or any way you please. No other book will ever be to him the wholly meaningless waste which it is even to his poor brother who has had the *Yan chi ch'o* bawled at him till he knows the sounds by heart, but the sounds only. Our boy can never open any book without finding on every page scores of his little stock of characters, out of which it is hard but he will hammer some sense for the rest. His stock is not large, but an enlarged edition of the Hornbook, based on a selection of six or seven hundred characters, would still be mastered with much less difficulty than the time-honoured *Sâm Tsz King.*

Of course there are objectors. To what are there not objectors? If you wish thoroughly to appreciate the number of fanciful objections of which human ingenuity is capable, just try to reduce some hoary difficulty—to make that easy which has always been hard, and, the objector thinks, always ought to be. Shew a good skater, for instance, an easy method of learning to skate, or a good swimmer an easy way of learning to swim. He doesn't see the necessity for it—is bound to confess he can't see where the difficulty is—thinks it very German—is sure the learner would pick up shocking bad form, &c., &c. I imagine the man who hit on the idea of alphabetising the margin of a book, for ready reference, felt rather proud of his invention; I am certain that nine out of ten of those to whom he shewed it threw cold water on his hopes. For their part they never experienced any difficulty in finding what they wanted, could find it in fact much quicker their own way than on this newfangled plan. It was ingenious no-doubt, and pretty to look at, but it wouldn't do for practical work. Then they would point out to him, with the most candid kindness, how dirty and dogs-eared the letters got by and by, and how they presently wore off altogether. At every mistake which occurred they would say, "Aha! this is your precious new system!" A very great deal of the furious opposition to chloroform, which raged just after its discovery, proceeded no doubt from the conviction, on the part of elderly and healthy surgeons, who had never suffered anything worse than a headache, that good, sound, honest pain (say an amputation or two) was a wholesome old institution, not to be trifled and made away with by a lot of these young fellows. They didn't see, themselves, what patients wanted with chloroform!

In native teachers this conservatism of abuses is apt to take the form of that latent wickedness which leads grown-up people to revenge needless sufferings of their youth by inflicting the like on their own or other folks' children. How many thousands of poor little creatures are dragged out of bed at five all the year round, made to wash in icy water, to eat fat, to hear long sermons, not because their elders really believe these things are good for them, but because they themselves went through the mill, and are determined that everybody else shall go through it. How much profitless work and admittedly useless drudgery is daily inflicted on various unfortunates all over the world, on no more rational pretence than that of, *I* had it to do! And when certain classes of people see things abolished only because they are useless, or made plain only because there is no reason why they should be crooked, their great resource is to cry out that the country, or the service, or the cause, or the rising generation, as the case may be, is going to the devil. I fear it must be written down as a law of human nature, *Few like to see that made easy which in their time was hard.*

So there are, and will be, persons who regard Mr. Piton's Hornbook as interesting and ingenious, but not more practically important than those reconstructions of the Chinese language in which almost every student indulges within his first year, and which would be so useful if only four hundred millions of people would adopt them. For my own part, I confess I regard the little book with the most sincere and unfeigned admiration. Side by side with it on my table lies the newspaper account of the opening of the Shanghai and Woosung Railway—of the two facts, I am not sure that the book is least important. Like all discoveries of the right way it is so eminently simple, that it may seem to some the idea has occurred to them again and again. The only wonder is that it should not have effectively occurred to anyone before.

One objection and one only have I heard which is entitled to an answer. It is this; —what is easy to us is not easy to Chinese, who often prefer their own more complicated way of stating or arranging facts, &c. That is no doubt quite true, but we might make the proposition more general, and say, what is easy to us is not easy to *children*, &c. Only very long practice can ever anticipate the queer and inexplicable way in which a child will regard the simplest fact.* The teacher has repeatedly to wonder at the curious difficulties children invent in a lesson he would have called easy, and at the absolute ease with which they master a lesson that he calls hard. But nevertheless certain cardinal facts of human nature remain, and they are true in China as in England. One column of the Multiplication Table is easier to learn than three, and five characters are more readily committed to memory than fifty. The general principles of teaching are founded on laws of the human mind; laws which operate wherever

---

* Hence partly the popularity of what is called pupil-teaching, a good enough system under (what it seldom, if ever, gets) plenty of adult superintendence and correction, otherwise most delusive.

the sun shines. It is this which makes the
"exact contrary" theory such wretched
nonsense, for, if everything in China *were*
the exact contrary to what it is in the west,
instead of beginning with our pupils in the
easiest book obtainable, we should begin
with the hardest; we should find that a
repetition of the same fact would only
weaken our boys' recollection of it, and that
to go over a lesson several times would
ensure its being forgotten altogether! In
place of anything so preposterous, we find
the Chinese themselves using and believing
a literal rendering of our own proverb,
Practice makes perfect. An easy sentence
in English may not make an easy sentence
in Chinese, but a method which is easy and
rational has an equal advantage over what
is clumsy, perverse, and irrational, whether
the vehicle of expression be Chinese, English, or Patagonian.

Whatever progress may be made in the
education of Chinese, or in the provision of
elementary and other books for them, nothing is so important as finding them the
means of easily learning to read. An American writer says that to give a boy a lesson
in history or geography is like cutting down
a tree for a settler in the woods, but that to
perfect your boy in reading is like *giving
the settler an axe.* So it is, and Mr. Piton
has done a good work well, a work that "is
great because it is so small." Abandoning,
and probably gladly abandoning the immense question of Tweedledum versus Twee-
dledee to his brethren of other communions,
who may be trusted to continue it with
the urbanity and taste which has hitherto
distinguished them, Mr. Piton has only, like
the modest author of the native Primer,
"left a little book to teach children."

L. C. P.

THE LAW OF INHERITANCE.

DECISION OF LIU-HUANG-CHUNG, PREFECT
OF FOOCHOW.

Inheritance—Religious Trusts.

The dispute between Yang-hung and
Chang-mou appears to be really as to who
should be considered Yan nah (or Patron) of
the Foo-tang-tzŭ, the other matters having
flowed in. The temple appears from the
records to have been built by one of the
Yang family, the character Yang having
been introduced into its name to bring them
good luck. It appears also that it was
subsequently repaired by one Chang, who,
having endowed it with lands, claims to be
considered in consideration thereof to be considered Yan nah, has altered the character
Yang in the name and drawn up new records.

Now it is evident that there cannot be two
lords in one temple without continual dis-
putes and that one good deed would be the

foundation of endless misfortune [if this
were sanctioned]. I decree therefore that
the temple belong to the Yang family, that
Chang take his endowment back again and
sell it or give it to somebody else; and as I
doubt, seeing that he got a rent from the
priests of Tls. 3.20 annually, that his gift
was altogether a free and generous one, I
order him to be flogged.

NOTE.—The foundation of a temple giving
the right of patronage to the founder and
his heirs, their right cannot be evaded by
subsequent benefactors, although these will
be allowed to recall their benefactions if
the consequent privileges of patronage are
denied them.

The summary way in which the unsuc-
cessful party to the suit is sentenced to
corporal correction on apparently general
principles seems rather arbitrary, but in point

of fact the flogging being redeemable by a small fine, it amounts to very much the same as a decree of costs against him.

JUDGMENT OF CHI-URH-CHIA, COMMISSIONER OF YEN CHOW.

Religious Trusts,—Alienation of Trust Property.

In this case Yang-shih-chin is the purchaser by regular sale, witnessed by formal deed, of eighteen mow of valuable land belonging to one Sung; it appears moreover that the land has passed through at least three hands, Sung having purchased it of one Fang, and it is alleged that it before this was owned by one Hsiang and granted by him to the Kao-lûng monastery.

The black-frocked gentry however held their tongues when Fang took possession of the property, and it is only now after twenty years have elapsed that a wandering bonze Chao-hsi, combining with a disreputable associate Hsiang-hsio-cheng, makes an attempt to get violent possession of the property.

The case has been decided by the Magistrate, but his decision not giving satisfaction the case is brought in appeal by Shih-chin.

In the first place, having given valuable consideration for the property, Yang cannot be said to have wrongfully seized it.

Secondly — If it be alleged that Sung had no deeds to shew for his possession, the priests would have been in much the same position as to proof of title, seeing they gave no consideration for the property.

Thirdly—Chao-hsi does not appear to be the regular representative of the Brotherhood and has no right to appear in the action.

We cannot reconcile the ignorance of the right to the land at the time it was alienated and the knowledge now—the ignorance of those primarily interested and the knowledge of their descendants, the ignorance of Fang's wrongful title and the knowledge of Sung and Yang's wrongful titles ; and the conduct of the shaveling, not contented with the six mow he had got, in seizing the opportunity to obtain violent possession of

twelve mow more, is abominable and deserving of punishment.

We decree therefore that the Magistrate's decision be reversed, and for the nonce holding Buddha's staff for him order the bald-headed reprobate to be severely flogged.

NOTE.—Purchaser of trust property for valuable consideration and without notice will not be disturbed if those interested had ample opportunity to oppose the transfer if they saw fit to do so. But inferentially a defective title would not hold if the rightful proprietors represented the matter within reasonable time. Also a bequest to a monastery or temple will be interpreted as a bequest to the priests specially attached thereto and their successors on the spot, not to the Church generally. The decision would possibly have been different if the temple had been endowed coupled with a condition to maintain ancestral worship and had one of the family interested come forward to protest against the alienation.

DECISION OF FANG-CHAO-TSUN, MAGISTRATE OF LE-SHUI.

Trusts.

Property devised with condition of maintaining ancestral worship cannot be alienated.

In this case the Chên family had seventy mow of land dedicated to the maintenance of ancestral worship, each in turn having the management of the sacrifices. This had continued from time immemorial, the provisions of the founders of the family being such that it was impossible for any unfilial son or careless grandson to divert the land to other uses though the family continued for one hundred generations. Suddenly an old but reprobate graduate Chên Chi-yi, disregarding the pious intentions of his ancestors, greedily and avariciously tries to appropriate twenty mow to his own ends. This was foolish, for his grey hairs were many ; he was like a burnt-out censer, a night when day is about to appear ; little earthly enjoyment was before him, and dead he would not have lost the property, for if he died without children would he not in the next world have fared with the rest of his ancestors, sharing alike with them the common provision for their spirits ? And although Chén Akwang be a widow, yet she is a member of the Chén family, and is asserting the great principle that the Ancestral worship of the family should not be neglected.

We decree therefore that the trusteeship go on as before, each in turn taking it, and that the tenants pay no heed to the terms of the underhand lease.

The offender ought to be punished, but in consideration of his age and poverty we excuse him his disrespect of his ancestors.

DECISION OF YEN HSIAO-HSÜ, MAGISTRATE OF SHAO-YANG.

Religious Trusts.

The object of a trust being still carried out the trust will be maintained.

In this case Lo Chi-su, a compound of wolf and tiger, already convicted at the Prefecture of poisoning the country with his venom on pretence of redeeming his offence, makes a fraudulent representation claiming a piece of land forming part of the demesne of the Hsing-lung monastery as established by an inscription on stone of long standing, and the services of which are still maintained (the monastery having been burnt) by the priest Tsung-chen in a mat-shed known as the Lei-chia-chung farm, representing further that it had been sold to him by a person against whom he has a spite, one Peng-chien-i.

Now supposing the sale to have been regular he has no right to vent his spite on Buddha, and his conduct in going on from injuring common people to attacking the priests, and not satisfied with snapping at men trying to bite at Buddha, shews that the punishment inflicted by the Prefect was not enough to frighten him ; we must try therefore if the cangue will have any effect.

NOTE.—Peng-chien-i it would appear was the person entitled to alienate supposing the trust to have lapsed, but it is laid down that so long as the objects of the original trust are carried out, it will be maintained even against the representatives of the original grantors. Had the services been given up the decision I am informed would have been different. Note the weight given to the record of the original trust engraved subsequently on a stone tablet.

DECISION OF MAO-TIEN-LAI, PREFECT OF PING-YANG.

Inheritance.—Land Tenure.

In this case Tsao-hsio is uterine brother of Tsao Che-hsien. Hsien appears to be childless and in easy circumstances, Hsio to have two children and to be utterly devoid of property, and covetous therefore of the valuables his brother may leave behind him. Hsien selling a piece of land belonging to him to the Military Doctor Le Hung-pao, Hsio holding that his brother's property is his, outrageously prevents Pao enclosing it, and Pao brings an action against him ; before this is decided Hsio tries to influence me [to decree] that Chi-hsien dying childless his property goes to his brother. Hsien however happens to be alive, and Hsio has therefore no claim, and for attacking the purchaser when his attempt to get his brother's land from him has failed he must be flogged.

NOTE.—This case lays down that a brother inherits when the deceased is childless, but that although heir he cannot prevent his brother aliening his property while living, as he could have stopped the sale ; had his brother inherited the land coupled with the condition of maintaining the ancestral sacrifices whether this condition had been specific or merely to be implied, the plaintiff seems to have thought himself justified in preventing the transfer, though there was no such condition on the simple ground of the injury to his prospects thereby.

DECISION OF LIU TIEN-YU, MAGISTRATE OF
YAO-CHOW.

Purchase for valuable consideration.

Wei Chêng-pu some years back appears to have purchased a piece of waste land from Chen-huang-le without any claim being raised by Huang Chih-chia, who now at length comes forward as owner of the property and builds a house on it.

In support of his claim he produces an unregistered deed drawn up at the end of the Ming dynasty the seal on which appears to be of the present dynasty, which can scarcely be accepted. However as Chi-chia is a poor scholar we direct Wei Cheng-pu to give him taels two as a charity, and at the same time the deed must be destroyed lest it be brought in question hereafter.

———

NOTE.—The title of a purchaser for valuable consideration will not be disturbed save on the clearest evidence, and doubtful documents calculated to afford ground for litigation will be ordered to be destroyed if the Court thinks them insufficient proof of the claim based on them. Inferentially it is however laid down that on clear evidence of plaintiff's title the purchaser would have had to give way.

Note also that a seal subsequently affixed will not be considered sufficient authentication of a document, and the disinclination to admit deeds executed previous to the commencement of the present dynasty.

———

JUDGMENT OF LI WEN-CHANG, DEPUTY SALT
COMMISSIONER OF THE LEANG-HUAI.

Testamentary disposition upheld on cause shewn.

In this case Yung Jih-hsin, the deceased, the son-in-law of Wang-Ming-wo, left a son Yung Yi-lang, and it is established that Ming-wo was a person of vile reputation.

On the approach of death Jih-hsin appears to have been very anxious regarding the unprotected state in which he was leaving his son, for although willing to entrust his care to his mother-in-law, he was afraid to leave the property in charge of his father-in-law, apprehending as has happened that he would sell it; and he was wise, for as a son is the best judge of his father so is a son-in-law of his father-in-law.

Jih-hsin therefore left his son to the care of his wife's family, but falsely representing that he had sold it all left his property secretly in trust to his friend Fang Yung-jen.

Ming-wo, however, heard of it and at once reclaimed it from him, and in three years it was all made away with as his son-in-law had anticipated.

If we excuse Ming-wo's disregard of his son-in-law as a person outside his family he should still have had consideration for this son left by his dead daughter ; and can this son, who having lost his mother when three months and his father when four years old, and being entirely dependant on these few mow of land for food, raiment and marriage, be satisfied now all is dissipated and he has nothing left to cling to ?

It appears that that portion of the estate that has been sold is utterly gone, but about half the property has been mortgaged and can be recovered. We decree therefore that Ming-wo's property be disposed of and applied to its redemption, that it be given to Fang Yung-jen in trust for the orphan as his friend desired, and be handed over to Yi-lang when he comes of age, and we order that Ming wo be flogged for disregarding the dead and injuring the living.

NOTE.—Relatives are the natural guardians of children left orphans, but if it is shewn that they are unworthy of the trust, a testamentary disposition giving the guardianship to a stranger will be upheld, otherwise it would appear the trustee so appointed would not resist their assuming the guardianship and taking possession of the property.

Note also that the purchasers of the alienated property in this case are not disturbed, although it is admitted the land was improperly made away with.

A CHINESE DICTIONARY IN THE CANTONESE

DIALECT.

A Chinese Dictionary in the Cantonese Dialect. Part I. A to K. With Introduction. By ERNEST JOHN EITEL, Ph.D. Tübing. London: Trübner & Co. Hongkong: Lane, Crawford & Co. 1877.

During the last few years, the means at the disposal of students for the effective study of the Chinese language and literature have been greatly increased. Chinese studies have been making vast and rapid strides in all departments of research. Here a philosophical translation; there a collection of Proverbial lore; from one scholar a learned work on philology: from another, the rhymes and songs of primeval China: even the very Japanese have entered the lists for sinological honours, for from Tokei, a map of China has been published, which, for beauty of execution and excellence of finish fairly rivals the productions of Perthes and Kupert. There is now no obstacle in the way to Chinese study, the facilities are ample though the encouragement is infinitesimal. When we compare the present state of affairs with what it was some forty or fifty years ago, we may well congratulate ourselves on the change. Books then were few and costly. Then the East India Company were almost the only patrons of literature in the far East, as many valuable works now extant abundantly show. For example, they defrayed the expenses of the publication of Dr. Morrison's Dictionaries which amounted to $60,000. Nor must we forget that after their day had passed, Chinese studies were munificently fostered by the merchant princes who succeeded. If men worked, money was forthcoming to defray the expenses of publication. But still the workers were hampered with the impedimenta of daily duty, for no man in China can devote himself to a literary life, however arduous, with the hope of living by it. *Fama* and *fames* go too much together. To adopt the words of Macaulay, with a slight variation—"The patronage of the public does not yet furnish the means of comfortable subsistence, and Chinese Scholars do not find munificent encouragement in Albemarle Street or Paternoster Row."

It is therefore highly honorable to the Hongkong Government and the Chamber of Commerce in continuance of these traditions to have granted Dr. Eitel the material assistance, without which the work now about to be reviewed could not have been published. The policy of such grants is far-sighted, as the results which have ensued to commercial and social interests sufficiently show; and it is equally honourable to Dr. Eitel, who, in his leisure hours, with characteristic energy has devoted himself to a tedious and enervating study in a climate disastrous to health, without the slightest prospect of pecuniary reward.

This work was urgently required. The original Tonic Dictionaries had reached fancy prices, and were kept under lock and key by their fortunate owners; they were handed round as a curiosity and regarded with looks of envy. Godowns were ransacked for this hidden treasure, and a solitary long-forgotten box rewarded the search. This supply was soon exhausted. Dr. Eitel then, recognizing the necessity of immediate action, forthwith formed the idea of issuing a new and revised edition. Two years' revision however satisfied him, that the work, in order to bring it down to the present state of Chinese scholarship, would require to be entirely re-cast. A new plan was therefore devised; the result being an essentially new Dictionary based on the work of Kanghi, the Indexes to Legge's Classics, Williams' Dictionary and other authorities. Although based on these authorities, it is quite an independent work, as the most cursory comparison of the pages of the new dictionary with the original one will suffice to show. It is not a supplement, or only one in the sense that the English Dictionaries of Latham and Webster are supplements to the original Johnson: Dr. Williams represents what was known of the Cantonese dialect twenty years ago; Dr. Eitel, what is now known of the language, after a period of unwonted literary activity.

Having thus shown the relation to which the present work stands to its predecessor, it now devolves upon me to indicate what the new plan and improvements are. In the first place, instead of having the phrases belonging to religion, the Classics, literature and the arts, colloquial and slang mixed up together, an arrangement has been made whereby they are grouped under several distinct heads; and their various subdivisions, such as Buddhism, Tauism, Technology and local phrases purely Cantonese are distinguished by having appropriate abbreviations attached to them. That there is still room for improvement even in this arrangement Dr. Eitel himself would be the first to admit. It is not too much to expect that the definitions in Kanghi might have been also classified and condensed, instead of following the very promiscuous arrangement of that most unmethodical work. The aim of the present undertaking should be more to supplement Kanghi than to act as a Handbook to it. It should have been Eitel upon Kanghi. If these Editors followed a historical system of collation it is often unapparent to sense; it seems to me (I speak under correction) that they were singularly free from that scientific and cultivated caution which is absolutely necessary to the composition of a philological work. They had it is true a principle of verifying their words with quotations, but even then this was followed out in a slip-shod sort of way, and the suitability of word to quotation is often far from being correct, and the quotation so garbled as to be unintelligible. Having no method, they were like men struggling through the darkness without a torch. That these things are so it is evident from the manner in which the work was compiled. By an Imperial mandate, twenty-seven of the most distinguished literati, members of the Hanlin, were requested within five years to complete a work, in which "No meaning should be left unexplained, as well as no sound omitted." When finished, it was revised by two, and a third was added to "superintend the press." The result is a work, the most remarkable ever compiled by an Asiatic race. There is, to quote Dr. Morrison, however "a want of unity and perspicuity in it. The student is sometimes referred backwards and forwards without finding satisfaction anywhere," &c. It is therefore surprising that Dr. Eitel should have followed the meanings of this work seriatim without classification. There were two courses open; first, either to group the analogous meanings i. e. those varying slightly together, with a grammatical subdivision; or second, group those meanings which are only employed in ancient literature, and those which are used in both modern and ancient literature. For instance, even at the risk of being sneered at like the simpleton with his muster brick, let the single character 之 be taken,—a bucketful of water from the ocean gives a pretty fair specimen of the whole. Well for 之, we find Kanghi gives the following fourteen explanations,

出 也, 是 也, 適 也, 往 也, 於 也, 語 辭, 此 也, 變 也, 至 也, 遺 也, 姓, 通 作 至, 本 是 芝 字. Of these, Dr. Eitel explains the first twelve seriatim thus :—

之 [i.w. 旃 ₍chin₎] K. to issue, thus, to come, go, with regard to, a mere expletive particle; this, these; to change; until; to transmit; a surname.

Being a particle, the meanings of 之 do not come under the first classification so obviously as a word possessing a larger range of meanings would, but that they are capable of being so classified, one has only to try to be convinced. With regard to the second classification into meanings ancient and modern, the distinction can be more easily made, for seven of the *above are only to be found in Ancient Books, but which are they? In the 禮 記 I find the following passage 延陵季子曰若魂 氣則無不之也. Now, which of the twelve meanings or so given by Dr. Eitel am I to select? I have no principle of selection; but if I were limited to such and such meanings as are used in the 禮 記 and contemporaneous books, I would be greatly assisted; but as it is now, I am open to choose the one which hits the idea I have formed of the sentence, a principle of selection highly dangerous and open to error, as every one, who has tried to translate without a teacher or translation, knows to his own sorrow, how apt we are to read into Chinese texts our own conceptions. I recommend neither one classification nor the other. Each seems to have its own peculiar advantages and disadvantages, but what I do contend for is that some classification is better than none, even if it were only to economize space by the exclusion of synonyms or to get rid

* See Dr. Morrison in loco.

of the "chaotic Confusion" (the phrase is Dr. Eitel's) which characterizes the arrangement of Kanghi.

By the way, the meaning of 之 over the phrase quoted above is given in Kanghi by the words 適 往, which, as readers will perceive, are rendered by "to come, go." I am open to conviction, but I do not think either 之 or 適 can derive the meaning of "to come" from the phrase in question. Besides, on reference to the commentary on the 禮 記, I find that the commentator, in the most emphatic language, expressly precludes the idea of coming or returning. 則 無不之適者, 言無所不之 適, 上或適於天, 旁適四方, 不可再反, the idea being it seems to me that the soul extends in every direction, in fact that it is all-pervading.

As one translation of the synonyms of a character may give a misleading idea as to the general scope, I will, in order to make the idea more explicit, give two more characters, chosen at random, from which, readers can verify their appositeness for themselves.

鈔 [a.w. 摲 ₍cháu₎ 抄 ₍cháu₎] K. read ch'áu take with a fork, mark off, collect taxes (by force); a surname, to copy, compel; read ch'au' paper money; a stamped receipt s.a. 抄 ch'au'; the end, deep or far, read ch'ui to take.

The following is from Kanghi = 又 取. 略 或 作 摲. 又 作 抄. 又 姓. 謄 寫. 強 鈔 引. 鈔 關. 同 抄. 末 深 遠. 取.

慶 K. read K'ing' (hing') congratulate, good, to praise, happiness, give, an expletive particle (=happily), name of a department, a surname, read k'ing virtue, determination.

慶 has the following synonyms in Kanghi, of which the above are the translation 賀 善 休 福 賜 發 語 詞 州 名, 又 姓. The last two meanings of Dr. Eitel I cannot find in Kanghi.

Under 鈔, I may note that the meaning to "mark off" though one of the meanings of 略 is certainly not one of the meanings of 鈔, as the phrase in Kanghi clearly shows. This meaning is therefore misleading and should be omitted. The idea of 略 here is somewhat analogous to the next meaning. One cannot translate 攻鈔 郡 縣 by "to mark off a township" when the idea is rather to seize a city by force. De Guignes *in loco* gives rapere, enlever.

Another feature, worthy of notice, is the Analysis of every character Dr. Eitel has made. He gives the number of the radical under which it is found in Kanghi, and also the number of strokes which go to form the primitive. To beginners, this is a great boon. It is an innovation which I have not hitherto noticed in any Anglo-Chinese Dictionaries whatever. Of course, as in any other study there is no "Royal road" to Chinese; beginners must get up their radicals, they must be able to identify them, to count their strokes, and to write them. The radicals must be assimilated to the beginner's mental organism before any substantial progress in character can be made; but to remember the order in which they occur is one of the greatest tasks which can be imposed on the memory. Now, when students are under the necessity of consulting Kanghi or any other dictionary native or foreign, which follows the same plan, the key is before him—the radical and strokes tells him almost the very page and part of the page where the character for which he is on the outlook, is to be found. The absence of these index numbers, when a character is used twice, indicates that its present sound or tone is derivative, not original.

The various contractions vulgar or obsolete characters, and differences in pronunciation as given in Kanghi are bracketed immediately to the right of the authorized character.

It is however a question, whether the time and the space expended have resulted in proportionate advantages; whether effec-

tiveness and simplicity have not been sacrificed to completeness, whether the stripling David has not been borne to the earth under the armour of Saul. However advantageous it may be to the comparative philologist to have all the growths and excrescences, the morphology and archaeology of a language or dialect presented before him, yet to practical Students of Chinese, who are after all the class that use Anglo-Chinese Dictionaries, and who have distractions enough, such numerous details can only be misleading and disheartening. Embarrased, bewildered, they stand amidst a profusion of philogical wealth which will take them years of study to appreciate. We are told " that this Dictionary confines itself entirely to the sounds of the Cantonese dialect as heard in Canton city." Well, so be it, but until now, on one of the best authorities, we were led to understand that the Cantonese dialect was the most regular of the Chinese dialects; if such irregularities characterize the most regular dialect, we wonder what irregularities are to be found in the others. However, here we are informed that within three miles of Shamin, that such and such a character is pronounced so without a change of meaning; that another is correctly pronounced in quite another way, a third character has got distinct names and two distinct intonations, a fourth is wrongly pronounced in such a way, while the fifth has its ancient lineage clearly stated. Enormous labour this! Cui bono! What does it matter to students of English, who only want to acquire the language as spoken in the educated and well-bred circles of the metropolis, that Shakespeare and the late Premier prefer revènue to rèvenue, that some people pronounce neither, nēēther, and others nīther, that curates and lawyers have vagaries of intonation and pronunciation peculiar to themselves, and that multitudes of most respectable people can never cease "exasperating" their "Hs." There are few beyond, say, Dr. Edkins in Peking, Mr Chalmers in Canton and Dr. Eitel himself, ripe scholars all three, who have or will have the slightest interest in these differ-ences of Chinese words. The great majority, like Gallio, care for none of these things. These collections are thoroughly compiled, and the highest credit is due, but an appendix or a separate monograph is the proper place for them; they are most valuable matter in the wrong place; they are here an encumbrance and are to be judiciously ignored.

In a further examination, for the work deserves the credit of a thorough one, I noticed an inconsistency for which I can find no rational explanation. I refer to the manner in which classical, geographical and personal names are spelled. The system here followed is that of Sir William Jones, according to which a considerable number of languages and dialects have been romanized. I believe that the multitudinous dialects of India, the Mandarin, the Fuchau and Cantonese dialects of China, the languages of the South Pacific and of the North American Indians have all been reduced according to this system. But our compiler, instead of sticking closely to the system which he has adopted, goes off at a tangent when he has a word to give in Mandarin, and follows the orthography of Dr. Morrison. Sir William's is good enough for the local dialect, while Dr. Morrison's is reserved for the honour of the official language. Thus, to be consistent 周, which we find as " Chow " should be written " Cheu " according to Sir William Jones' system; 楚 Ts'oo instead of Ch'u; 書, when speaking of the Shu King, we find Shoo instead of Shu. Nor is Dr. Eitel even consistent in this, for when speaking of the Shi King 詩, where we should have expected She, Shi is found instead; again 鱺諸, an old Chinese Nero, is written in conformity with Sir Wm. Jones' not with Dr. Morrison's. Several other examples can be cited for which I can find no satisfactory reason. Both systems seem to be used indiscriminately. Perhaps a desire to retain the old orthography of the early

missionaries ; or to facilitate reference to Morrison, Medhurst and Legge was the cause. Perhaps Dr. Eitel was actuated by the same sense of conservatism which the Anglo-Indians possessed, when the British Government systematized the geographical names throughout India ; when Juggernaut, Cawnpore, Lucknow, Masulipatam, all names of special or historical interest and whose very spelling is encrusted in our literature, were changed into Jagannath, Kanhpur, Lukhnau and Machlepatnam! The Anglo-Indians had some faint reason for the outcry, loud and deep, which they raised against the change involving a change of historical identity. But the the reason for the retention of the old names alongside another system in this work I fail to see. Surely not an aid to perspicuity!! In a dictionary of all books, and in Chinese of all languages, the strictest orthographical uniformity should be observed. The spelling of words like Chow and Ts'oo are not identified in so marked a manner with foreign progress in China, as the spelling of Indian names with the growth of British power in India, that system must be sacrificed for them ; and besides when we remember, that the absence or presence of a " spiritus asper," of a diacritical mark of a tone, makes an entirely different word, it is essential that unnecessary variations of all kinds should be as few as possible. The evil is a growing one ; the most cursory inspection of the pages of this *Review*, of its Missionary contemporary *The Recorder*, will show the necessity—as Mr. Chalmers has elsewhere indicated—of having a uniform system, which all can follow and all can understand.

With regard to dialects Dr. Eitel on the whole follows Edkins. At the commencement of the Christian Era, it is supposed that, instead of the multiplicity of dialects which now exist, one common language was spoken by the entire people. This primeval language possessed all the leading characteristics of modern Chinese: it was monosyllablic, asperated, toned. It was from this tongue that Cantonese directly sprung. Cantonese retains more of its special features than any other of the modern dialects; the chief differences being a few consonantal changes from the soft to its corresponding hard sounds, and an increase in the number of the tones. Remarking on the very happy manner in which the position of the asperate is illustrated, and on the invaluable hints for discriminating peculiarly Chinese sounds, we will now pass on to the chapter on Tones.

This chapter is a most interesting one, inasmuch as it is the first attempt at an explanation of their origin and growth which has ever been published. The account of the origin however seems to me to be obscure and contradictory. There is neither logical nor historical sequence in the whole account, and Dr. Eitel himself seems to have felt it, for his verbiage, his tautology and his repetitions, so unlike his usual lucid manner, seem to indicate that he was floundering about in search of an idea which had eluded his grasp. How can he explain the following: "The Chinese language persistently retained its original monosyllabic character and gradually supplied the *want of an expansive stock* of syllables, in an equally effective though entirely unique manner, by means of intonations" (p. xix.), and again in pursuance of the argument or rather conjecture, we have "The Chinese were hard pushed to make the *naturally expansive stock* of syllables keep pace in its development with the written system" (p. xx.) I refer readers themselves to the passage; it seems to be a string of conjectures, which as soon as they are made are conveniently thrown overboard by some rhetorical reservation, such as "But, however that may be," "Anyhow" and so on. In order to understand the paragraph I analysed it, stripped it of its verbiage, and resolved it into the following propositions, which I think give a pretty fair idea of the original; it is however not improbable that the drift of it has been totally misunderstood, if so, it has not been

for the want of the requisite study and care.

1. Chinese language possibly poorer in vocables than other languages in a primitive state.

2. Probably so; but this however is certain that the monosyllabic Chinese language "gradually supplied the pressing want of an expansive stock of vocables by means of intonation, instead of agglutination and inflection."

3. Since an English child in China learns Chinese in a less time and with less difficulty than it could learn English at home in England, it therefore follows that the tones are as natural and practicable as grammatical inflections, and as equally devoid of mystery.

4. Using a symbolic system of writing with the spoken language *may have* aided to continue the monosyllabic form of the primitive spoken language and *may have* principally caused the avoidance of agglutination &c.

5. Anyhow: the Chinese language has succeeded by intonation in multiplying its vocables, while retaining its original monosyllables, and rejecting agglutination and inflection by reason of circumstances and innate tendency.

6. Seemingly the "first ancestors" had no idea of writing as they spoke; of making writing subservient to articulation.

7. On the contrary, they invented a pictorial system and continued its use, even when natural objects were exhausted; and ideas began to be delineated as if they were objects of mental visison rather than subjects of articulate speech.

8. Consequently writing developed faster than spoken language, and thus we can understand how "the Chinese were hard pushed to make the naturally expansive stock of syllables keep pace with its development."

9. The union existing between the written and spoken language is too natural a tie to be dissolved without destroying the practical use of one or the other of these social factors.

10. Now the Chinese language might have progressed to pollysyllabic speech if the written character had been susceptible of inflection and agglutination. This was not so.

11. There was ideographic writing capable of infinite increase; and there was the spoken language, poor in syllables, feeling under the necessity to enlarge its stock of syllables, and to coin new words in order to avoid a rupture.

12. Two alternatives open : either the written system would have to become alphabetic, or the spoken language agglutinative and inflective, the adoption of which would have made the rupture between written and spoken languages still more serious.

13. Hence the contrivance of tones is not unnatural, and may have been the instinctive following of the noises made by thunder, "windstorms," water, and animals.

Such is Dr. Eitel's present theory of the origin of the tones. I intended to attack nearly every proposition in detail, as it seems that here we have not only *petitiones principii, non sequiturs* and contradictions, but we have assumptions which directly violate the first principles of philology. As however this review is sufficiently long, I shall delay my criticism on this part of the question till the completion of the work, or till more leisure is at my disposal.

When we come to the history of the tones and to their variations, Dr. Eitel is himself again. He treads on the firm earth, he is not soaring amidst the nebulæ. Pages XXII-XXIX are eminently practical and highly suggestive. Dr. Williams has remarked that "Tones are an effort to avoid the confusion which must ensue in speaking many homophonous words in order to add to the accuracy of speech and facilitate conversation," and Dr. Eitel has illustrated this branch of his subject so clearly and has so completely systematized the tonal inflections that he deserves the hearty thanks of all students of Cantonese.

Before concluding, it is only right that a specimen of Dr. Eitel's manner of handling

a character should be given. I will therefore select one from the latter portion of the present instalment of the dictionary ; and in order to show the differences between this and several preceding works, I shall also affix what is said under the same character in these works.

Dr. EITEL, Hongkong, 1877.—

Cl.10

搖 K. to shake, grieved and having no confidant, to make, a surname; read *iá* to shake.—Cl. 中心 | | ˌchung ˌsām ˌiá ˌiá in my heart all agitated (*Shi.*)—Mi. | 動 ˌiá tung² shake, agitated (*K.*); 招搖 ˌchiú ˌiá star β in Bootes (*K.*), to give one's self airs (*Wade*); 扶 | ˌfú ˌiá a violent wind, rapid promotion (*K.*); 步 | ˌpö² ˌiá jewels on hair-pins (*K.*); 逍 | ˌsiá ˌiá soaring around (*K.*); 須 | ˌsü ˌiá momentarily (*K.*); 郁 | ˌiá yuk, vibrate ; 頭 ˌiá ˌt'au shake the head; | 鈴 ˌiá ˌling ring the bell.—Co. | | 擺擺 ˌiá ˌiá ˌpái ˌpái swinging, swaggering; | 下 ˌiá ˌha to dandle.

Dr. WILLIAMS, Shanghae, 1874.—

搖 From hand and a jar.

To move, to shake, to wag; to sway to and fro; agitated, tossed, vibrating; disturbed, discomposed.

| 櫓 to work a scull.

| 動 to joggle; to shake; waving to and fro, fluttering; unsteady; amazed, perturbed.

風雨所漂 | [my nest] is tossed by the wind and rain.

| 頭 to shake the head, to refuse.

扶 | 直上 rose directly to high rank, as if on a roc's back.

| | 擺擺 swaggering, proud.

| 鈴 to ring a hand-bell.

| 光 a revolving light; a twinkling, as of the stars.

| | 欲墜 it shakes as if just about to fall.

招 | 誘騙 者 those who have tried to pass themselves off [as rich men] by bragging.

Dr. CARSTAIRS DOUGLAS, London, 1873.—
iáu [*R.* to shake; to agitate,=col. *ió*] iáu-tŏng, agitated, excited and almost in commotion, as the people when hearing reports of rebellion, &c. *Tŏng-iáu* id. *iáu-tŏng jin-sim*, to disturb the minds of the people by such rumours. *iáu-tŏng bin-sim* id. *siun-iáu-tŏng*, making too great a display of one's wealth, so as to draw the notice of robbers or mandarins. *Chiau-iáu*, spreading rumours of what should not be spoken about, as of rebellion coming near, or about money or valuable goods in a house so as to incite robbery. *Chiau-iáu ni'u-bok*, to seduce people's ears and eyes, as great show of wealth attracting robbers, or as highly-adorned women alluring men.

MACLAY and BALDWIN, Foochow, 1870.—
搖 Also read *yeu²*; to shake, to move, to wave; to wag, as the head; agitated, disturbed; to make: 扶 | *ₛhú ₛyeu*, a violent wind; 須 | *ₛsü ₛyeu*, a moment; COM., | 動 *ₛyeu tong²* to move, disturb; to agitate (a matter); | 頭 *ₛyeu ₛt'au* to shake the head, as a sign of dissent; | 尾 乞 憐 *ₛyeu⁵mui k'éük*, *ₛling* "wag the tail and beg pity"—to act the sycophant; | 櫓 *ₛyeu ⁵lu*, to scull; | 會 *ₛyeu ₛgeu hwoi²* to shake (dice in order to draw one's share) at a mutual-aid club; COLL., | 錢 槇 *ₛyeu ₛchiéng ch'eu³* to shake "the cash-branch," as beggars do at new-year's.

Dr. WILLIAMS, Canton, 1856.—
搖 Moved, agitated, disturbed; to shake, to wag; to make; *ₛiú ⁵lò*, to work a scull; *ₛiú tung²* to move, to disturb, either mentally or physically; *ₛfú ₛiá*, a violent wind, to rise rapidly in office or rank; *ₛiú yuk₀* unsteady, not firm on it's base; *ₛiú ₛchung*, to ring a bell; *ₛiú ₛt'au* to shake the head, to refuse; *ₛiú ₛiú* disturbed, troubled; *ₛiú ₛiú yuk₀* not firm, unstable; *ₛiú ₛiú ⁵pái ⁵pái*, swaggering, proud.

Dr. MEDHURST, Macao, 1832.—
搖 Vulg. *yĕò*: to shake, to wave, to move backwards and forwards. Yaôu lâm, 搖 籃, *yeô ná*, a cradle. Hong é séy p'heaou yaôu, 風 雨 所 飄 搖 *hong hoĕ sey pheaou yĕò*; moved and agitated by the wind and rain.

Dr. MORRISON, Macao, 1819.—
搖 From hand and a pitcher: the mind agitated without having any one to trust to. To shake; to move; to wave; to imitate. *Foo Yaou* 扶 | a violent wind. *Chaou yaou* 招 | the name of a star. *Seu yaou* 須 | a moment of time. *Poo yaou* 步 | an ornament for the head. *Yaou kwang* | 光 vibrating light; certain stars. *Yaou pae* | 擺 swaggering strut. *Yaou show* | 手 to wave the hand. *Yaou tung* | 動 to move, either morally or physically. *Yaou too* | 頭 to shake the head: denoting disapproving or denying. *Yaou yaou* | | a proud gait.

M. de GUIGNES, Paris, 1813.—
搖 Agiter, remuer.

Agitare, movere, commovere. *x-kouâng*, vel *tchao-x*, septima stella in constellatione ursæ minoris seu currûs polaris; *tcháo-x*, inquietus, perturbationes excitare; *x-hoĕ*, perturbare; *x-x-paÿ paÿ* dicitur de incessu superbo, quo quis ambulans vestes et corpus agitat.

Besides presenting a highly valuable comparison, supplementing the work of the critic and affording the reader an opportunity of judging for himself, these specimens show pretty accurately the advances which foreigners have made in Chinese lexicography, more especially during the last seven years; and they also show that the present work is not a whit behind any of its predecessors, in scholarship, in comprehensiveness and in practical utility. No one is able to look over the pages of this dictionary without being struck at the large amount of labour and research which it must have entailed. The book is needed more than ever, for the time is now come when the merchant and tradesman, if they are to hold their own, must set themselves to learn the dialect along with the diplomatist, the missionary and the Customs official. With steady and unshrinking perseverance the native is competing with the foreigner in every department of commercial enterprise. They have carried the war into the enemy's country. They act now on the offensive; and an ever increasing hostility makes it every day more difficult to withstand them. It is useless to cry for increased commercial rights when our sheer ignorance of the language prevents us from availing ourselves of the rights we have. Commercial men, in this respect, may take a lesson from the missionary. They know their treaty rights. They go to their country congregations in the interior; but are commercial men competent to go to their silk and tea markets and read a native price current? It is self evident that unless we get rid of the army of middlemen, the trade will swerve more and more into Chinese hands. Our action must therefore be aggressive; and it cannot be so effectually without a knowledge of the language; and strange it will be, if, with the increased means which Dr. Eitel in the South has placed at our disposal, we cannot make it so.

ALEXANDER FALCONER.

SHORT NOTICES OF NEW BOOKS

AND LITERARY INTELLIGENCE.

Inaugural Lecture, on the constituting of a Chinese Chair in the University of Oxford; Delivered in the Sheldonian Theatre, October 27, 1876. By Rev. James Legge, M.A. Oxford, LL.D. Aberdeen, Professor of the Chinese Language and Literature. Oxford and London, James Parker and Co. London Trübner and Co., 57 and 59 Ludgate Hill, 1876.

The establishment of a Chinese Chair at the University of Oxford must rejoice the heart of every Englishman in China who desires to have higher reasons than those of commercial and political greatness for being proud of his country. It is almost unaccountable, if one comes to consider it, that whilst a "University" naturally might be expected to represent the learning of the whole universe, the greatest Universities of Great Britain, almost to the present day, represent adequately but the learning of two countries, Greece and Rome. "*Ex Oriente lux*" is a truth the recognition of which dates back much farther than the very history of the two most ancient Universities of England, and yet the study of Oriental Languages and Literature has, until quite recent times, been sadly neglected by both. Considering moreover, with special reference to China, the importance of the commercial interests England has here at stake, and the advantages to be derived politically from a mutual good understanding of the two countries, comparing also what other countries, especially France and Russia have done, in the way of constituting several Chinese Chairs, for the promotion of Chinese studies, it is but tardy and scanty justice that has been done to the demands of England's positive interests in China in founding the Chinese Chair at Oxford. Scanty we call this measure, because it is by no means to the credit of the wealthiest University of the world to exhibit its neglect of the language, literature, history, philosophy and religion of one fourth of the human race by establishing, almost reluctantly, a Chinese Chair whose endowment has to be provided for by "a public Subscription and the University conjointly."

The newly-installed Professor, Dr. Legge, who indeed was the fittest and most deserving occupant of the Chair established at last in Oxford, devoted almost the whole of his Inaugural Lecture to give the reasons for the constituting of his Chair. For this purpose he reviews the efforts hitherto made in Europe for the promotion of Chinese studies, referring to Professor Kidd, Dr. Morrison, Sir George Staunton, Professors Fearon, Summers and Douglas in England, to Professors Fourmont, Rémusat, Julien and d'Hervey de St. Denys in France, to Professor Schott in Berlin and the Chinese Chairs of Munich and Vienna, to Professors Hoffman and Schlegel in Leyden, Severini and Puini in Florence, Wassiljeff and Pestchuroff in St. Petersburg. With the same end in view, viz. to vindicate the constituting of the Chinese Chair at Oxford, Dr. Legge next surveys the relations at present subsisting between England and China, from a political, religious and commercial stand-point, and finally enters upon two other arguments which should long ago have brought such a Chair into existence, namely the history and literature of China and the nature of its language considered in themselves. After expressing his gratefulness to the first proposers of the Chair, to the President and Fellows of Corpus Christi College

and to the members of Council, Congregation and Convocation, who brought the thing to pass, Dr. Legge concludes by saying "what I can do, to justify their choice I will, with God's help, do, to the extent of my ability, both in the way of research and of teaching, the first object always being to make the Chair practically useful."

There is no doubt about this, that Dr. Legge will make his Chair practically useful, not only to Oxford and its reputation, but to England, and even to the world at large, by the mere continuation of his labours as the foremost and soundest translator and commentator of the Chinese Classics, and by the share he will take in the publication of the "Sacred Books of the East" as planned by Max Müller. There is however another way in which the Professor's learning might be utilized by his country, and it has been suggested to us by an allusion in Dr. Legge's Inaugural Lecture to the École Spéciale des Langues Orientales Vivantes in Paris. It appears that at this College in Paris a number of Oriental Languages are taught, each department being conducted by a French professor, assisted by a native scholar of the country the language of which is represented. "The provision thus made in Paris for the training of young men in a knowledge of Chinese and other Eastern languages is as complete as it well could be. When they have passed their examinations and received their diplomas, many of them go abroad to take part in the embassies and consulates of France or to assist in the promotion of its commerce,— having in the first place laid the foundations of both a scientific and practical knowledge of the chief instrument which they have to employ in the fulfilment of their duties."

There is nothing whatever to prevent the practical success of a similar plan, if introduced at Oxford and combined with the competitive system at present supplying officers for the Civil Service in Hongkong and the Consular Service in China. In a former review (see Vol. IV., page 302) we took the position that an English Professor at Oxford or London could indeed teach the syntax, prosody, history and literature of China, but would not be competent to teach the practical use of any one spoken dialect. But the whole of the objection we then raised would be obviated if a Professor of Chinese at Oxford or London were assisted by natives of China. Suppose, for instance, Professor Legge to have under his exclusive control two Chinese graduates, one a native of Peking, the other a native of Canton, and suppose a rule were made that every candidate for an appointment in the Consular Service in China and the Hongkong Civil Service had to qualify himself by two years' study of Chinese at Oxford under the superintendence of the Professor, we have no hesitation in saying such a plan would produce lasting benefit both to the Consular Service and to the Colony of Hongkong. Such a plan might be made to work still more effectively if Dr. Legge would receive a number of Chinese youths both from the North and South of China to avail of the advantages of an English University education under his superintendence, whose association with the candidates for the Consular Service and the Hongkong Civil Service would be an immense boon to all parties concerned.

We are glad to observe elsewhere that since the delivery of Professor Legge's Inaugural Lecture a Chinese Scholarship has also been established at Oxford. In a Convocation held on 15th November, 1876, a form of decree was passed accepting a gift from Sir John Francis Davis, Bart., K.C.B., D.C.L., of 1,666*l.* 33*s.* 4*d.* 3 per cent. Consols, for the purpose of encouraging the study of Chinese, in such a manner and subject to such regulations as the University shall from time to time determine.

The Chinese Recorder and Missionary Journal. November-December, 1876.

There is little to interest the general reader or Chinese student in this, from a Missionary point of view, tolerably interesting but rather dull number. Mr Phillips contributes a fourth chapter of his Zaitun researches, illustrated by a map of that part of the Fohkien province which was traversed by Marco Polo; and Dr Edkins gives a brief account of a visit he paid to the "Monastery of the Sandal-wood Buddha." The term question continues to exercise the minds of most of the contributors to this periodical.

The Far East. A Monthly Journal, published simultaneously in Tokio, Japan ; Shanghai, China ; and in Hongkong. New Series. Vol. 2. No. 1 & 2.

There is a pleasing variety of illustrations in the two numbers, especially in the first, the photographs of which are far superior to those of the second number. The portraits of Mr Medhurst, Mr Giquel, and Bishop Russell and the accompanying biographical notices are of permanent interest. The photograph of the compressed feet of a Chinese woman, however, does not add to the attractive features of the number in question, nor do we think the publication of the portraits of Japanese singing girls in good taste. Mr Stent contributes a poem entitled "Murder will out ;" Dean Butcher a lecture, recently delivered at Shanghai, on "The religious belief of ancient Greece." There is also a series of legends and tales from Japan, which deserve reading, but the rest of the letterpress scarcely comes up to the average.

Conchyliologie Fluviatile de la Province de Nanking. Par le R. P. Heude, de la Compagnie de Jésus, Missionaire Apostolique au Kiang-Nan. Premier et deuxième fascicule. Paris. Librairie F. Savy, 77 Boulevard Saint-Germain.

The Reverend Father Heude, well known in Europe, among the admirers of mollusca, by his contributions to the *Journal de Conchyliologie*, furnishes in the two elegant brochures before us an important contribution to the Zoology of China. The sixteen-lithographed plates containing a series of thirty-six beautiful life-like representations of shells, principally varieties of the Unio, found by him in the rivers of Hoonan, and the adjoining provinces of Central China, are accompanied by a classified descriptive catalogue which is written in Latin. The measurements of each shell are given according to Crosse's system, whose terminology the learned author has adopted. The habitat of each shell is also specially stated in each case.

Bibliotheca Orientalis. A new catalogue of works on the history and languages of the East, etc., etc. By Bernhard Quaritch, 15, Piccadilly, London, 1876.

This is a supplement to the general catalogue for 1874, and contains among other articles one on China comprising the titles of 315 books or parcels of pamphlets on Chinese subjects. Most of these books are old works and some of them extremely rare. The prices affixed to these books on China are high and those of Chinese works out of all proportion with their cost in China.

Manners and Customs of the Chinese at Macao. Translated by Rufino F. Martins. Reprinted from the "Far East." Shanghai, 1877.

This is a very small book of very great pretensions. The preface informs us that "these papers have been translated *in part* from a work published in Macao in the year 1867, by Mr Manuel de Castro Sampaio, entitled Os Chins de Macao, and *dedicated to the Royal Asiatic Society,*" and further that "the greater portion of the interesting particulars were furnished by *the best Sinologues of Macao,* who took pains to revise the whole of the work." The translator further appends to the preface a page containing "*Opinions of the Press*" and having thereby learned to think himself a great public personage, he prefixes his photograph, with a red rose in each corner, as frontispiece to the pretentious little volume. So sure is he

moreover that the *China Review* will maintain him on his fancied pedestal of fame that he requests us to send him a couple of slips of the Review which we are to give his work, "that I can paste it in my book (opinions of the Press), and oblige."

It is impossible, without reference to the original, to say how much of the book under review belongs to Mr. Sampaio and how much or little to Mr. Martins. But the latter says in his preface that he "can vouch for the truth of all contained in this little volume," so we absolve Mr. Sampaio beforehand from what we may have to charge the little book with and throw the responsibility for all it contains on Mr. Martins.

It is a neatly-printed book, tastefully got up, and if we add that the paper is the best of the whole book, we have said about everything we can honestly say in its praise. The descriptions of the manners and customs of the Chinese of which the volume is made up are of the style and quality of the exercises which are written at any second rate school in Hongkong by a mediocre schoolboy, and the impression which a perusal of the whole gives of the manners and customs of the Chinese at Macao is for the most a caricature. The reader is, for instance, assured again and again that it is an established custom for the bridegroom on the occasion of his wedding to be helplessly drunk (p. 7, 9, 11), and on referring to a certain annual procession it is asserted (p. 52) that "the individuals who join in the procession are all intoxicated, as the procession will not come out unless the men are in this condition." Again, speaking of New Year's Day (p. 55), Mr. Martins says "this day is considered among them as a fast day (!) which, it is said, was established in order to avoid cases of intoxication." If this is the state of things among the Chinese at Macao, all we can say is that the Chinese of Macao are different from all the rest of the Chinese people, and Mr. Martins ought to have informed his readers of the fact. But we are inclined to think that Mr. Martins is not a sober observer. Almost everything he sees and fails to understand he styles ridiculous, even the funeral rites and the religions of the Chinese. The "sinologues of Macao" have evidently overlooked this part of the work. Nor could they perhaps be expected to be *au fait* in such affairs. But these "best sinologues of Macao," whoever they may be, ought certainly to have revised the literary information with which the book is freely interlarded, and which will be regarded as of the most novel kind anywhere outside Macao. We will give a few quotations:—

> P. 64. Kuantai was a famous warrior who had a large tree to which great virtues are attributed.
>
> P. 70. All cooking stoves have a god who accompanies them continually.
>
> P. 72. The prince Fuhy was the first individual who treated on the subject of medicine.
>
> P. 74. They cure all ordinary diseases easily, and ably attend to dislocations and fractures. . . . They have also no knowledge of surgery.
>
> P. 78. There are in China three principal religions. The first is that of Ju-chian, *worship of lawyers* . . . Its promoter is the emperor of the celestial regions.
>
> P. 80. They consider Kuanyn as the zealous advocate of the human daughters of the celestial regions.

By this last phrase Mr. Martins means Chinese women, and by the term "lawyers" he evidently refers to the literati of China. But these quotations, which are a fair sample of the mass of crude absurdities with which the little book is filled up, require no further comment. Mr. Martins' style is simply worse than Johnsonian. When referring to China he invariably uses the phrase "Celestial Regions." He prefers the word "Cephalalgy" to headache (p. 61), talks about "explanations found in clinic exercises" (p. 73), about "rats being generally confined to the poor class of courtezans

both ashore and afloat," and makes a whole procession "dissolve" in a new joss-house (p. 53). We regret we cannot contribute anything more flattering to Mr. Martins' book of "Opinions of the Press."

The Tokio Times, Vol. I., No. 1-8. Tokio, January 6 to February 24, 1877.

The first eight numbers of this new Journal before us are highly promising. Apart from the political and commercial intelligence to be found in this weekly periodical we have a series of articles interesting for diplomatists on the different legations in Japan, a contribution to ecclesiastical history " Japan and Rome in the seventeenth century," a lyric drama from the Japanese "the Deathstone," a review of the latest "English-Japanese Dictionary" published by Mr. Satow and Ishibashi Masakata, an essay on "the early study of Dutch in Japan," and two valuable articles on Japan and Corea. An interesting feature of each number consists also in the extracts given from native periodicals, and altogether this *Tokio Times* appears to come, in scope, style and general plan as a Journal for residents in Japan, very near to what the *Celestial Empire* is for China.

舊約詩篇 (*The Psalms of the Old Testament.* Translated in Cantonese Vernacular, 1876.)

聖日禱文 (*Collects, Epistles and Gospels of the Common Book of Prayer.* Hongkong, St. Stephen's Church, 1877.) Both of these books are translations (using the Chinese character) in the vernacular of the Canton province, prepared by the Rev. A. B. Hutchinson, Sec. C. M. S., Hongkong. Versions of both existed before in the bookstyle and in Mandarin Colloquial. Part of the second of the two books had also been previously translated in Cantonese vernacular by the Rev. G. Piercy and other Missionaries, but we find, on comparing Mr Hutchinson's version with the older ones, that he did not copy, but strove to improve upon them, and he has succeeded in this to a certain extent. We noticed a number of printer's errors caused no doubt by the distance from Hongkong at which the books were printed. As to the psalms Mr Hutchinson had no Cantonese version to go upon, and he certainly deserves high praise for the practically satisfactory solution of such a difficult problem as that of translating the Psalms of the Old Testament into readable and intelligible Cantonese Colloquial. We are no advocates of Colloquial versions, as it is our conviction that those who are able to read these versions are equally able to read the existing Delegates' version, which has the advantage of being not only in good Chinese style and taste, but especially also intelligible all over the Empire. For the purposes of the Church of England, however, Colloquial versions are indispensable, and those provided by Mr Hutchinson are equal to any we have seen.

The German Club Concordia.—A lecture on the life of the rebel emperor Hung Siuts'uen was delivered before the members of the Shanghai Club Concordia on 12th January. The lecturer traced, with the assistance of a large map specially prepared for the occasion, the history of the great rebellion, from its origin in Kwangtung and Kwangsi to its suppression by the capture of Nanking, the life and history of Hung Siuts'uen forming the prominent topic of a highly appreciated lecture.

The North China Branch R. A. S.—At a meeting of the Royal Asiatic Society in Shanghai, held on 22nd January, a paper, from the pen of Mr O. von Möllendorf was read "on the Vertebrata of the province of Chihli, with notes on their Zoological nomenclature." At another meeting of the same Society, held on 20th February, the newly elected President Mr Kingsmill delivered his inaugural lecture. The lecturer reviewed in a lengthy address, the delivery of which

occupied two hours, "the recent geological discoveries and opinions on the period immediately antecedent to History." That portion of the lecture which referred to the geology of the Central Asian plains and to the probable desiccation of the Siberian inland seas will be read with great interest if published in the Society's Journal.

COLLECTANEA BIBLIOGRAPHICA.

Das Ausland. No. 42. Die Ueberlandroute nach China über Assam.—No. 45. Zur Geschichte der Erforschung Tibets.

Magazin für die Literatur des Auslandes. 45 Jahrg. No. 44. Eine Landreise von Paris nach Peking. 2.—No. 45. G. Schlegel's chinesische Uranographie.—No. 46. N. Sewerzow's Erforschung des Thian-Shan Gebirgssystems und Dr. Petermann's Specialkarte.

Globus. Hrsg. von R. Kiepert. 30 Bd. No. 15-17. Eine Wanderung durch die chinesische Provinz Tschili im März 1874.—No. 20-24. A. Kohn, aus dem Reiseberichte Preschewalski's über die Mongolei und das Land der Tanguten.

Europa. Redig. von H. Kleinsteuber. No. 48. Aus West-China.—No. 50. Aus dem Religionscultus der Chinesen.

Westermann's illustrirte deutsche Monatshefte. Red. Ad. Glaser, October 1876. —II. Beta, Blicke auf Indo-China.

Allgemeine Zeitung (Augsb.) Beilage. No. 317-323. Aus Japan and China.

Illustrirte Zeitung. 67 Bd. No. 1743. In der Kirgisensteppe.

Wiener Abendpost (Beilage zur W. Zeitung). No. 260-261. Thierleben und Jagd in der Mongolei und Nordtibet.

Annalen der Hydrographie und maritimer Meteorologie. Hrsg. von der Kaiserl. Admiralität. 4 Jahrg. 12 Heft. 1876. Beschreibung . . . der neu eröffneten Häfen Hoi-how auf Hainan und Hai-phong in Tongking. Die neu eröffneten Häfen in China: Ichang, Wuhu, Wenchow, und Pei-bai (Pakhoi).

Allgemeine musikalische Zeitung. Red. Fr. Chrysander. No. 37-40. von Schafhäutl, über das Gut-Komm, eine chinesische viersaitige Laute, und über chinesische Musik.

Oesterreichische Monatsschrift für den Orient. 2 Jahrg. Wien, Dec. 15, 1876. No. 12. Beilage. Die Beurtheilung der Chinesen. Von Dr. Friederich Ratzel.

Literarisches Centralblatt. Hrsg. Prof. Dr. Fr. Zarncke. No. 47. Prof. W. W. Grigorjew, die Nomaden als Nachbarn und Eroberer civilisirter Staaten. —No. 48. The Chinese Classics. By J. Legge. Vol. III.

Zeitschrift der deutschen Morgenländischen Gesellschaft. Bibliographische Anzeigen. Georg von der Gabelentz: pag. 587. Stand und Aufgaben der chinesischen Lexicographie, als Anzeige zu Dr. Wells Williams' Syllabic Dictionary.—pag. 603. E. J. Eitel, Feng-shui, or the rudiments of natural science in China.

Pall Mall Budget, January 19, 1877. The land and the people of China.

The Celestial Empire. A Journal of native and foreign affairs in the Far East. Vol. VII., No. 26. Record of the Buddhistic Kingdoms.—Vol. VIII., No. 1. Chinese History. A Chinese poet. Record of the Buddhistic Kingdoms.—No. 2. The Empress and her premier. Record of the Buddhistic Kingdoms.—No. 3. The Duke of K'ung successor of Confucius. Record of the Buddhistic Kingdoms.—No. 4-6. Record of the Buddhistic Kingdoms.— No. 7. Women's secret societies. Record of the Buddhistic Kingdoms.—No. 8. Chinese prophecies. Confucius and Confucianism.—No. 9. Private proclamations. No. 9 and 10. The Border lands of Geology and History. By T. W. Kingsmill.

North China Daily News, Feb. 2, 1877. S. W. Bushell, a review of Frank's catalogue of oriental porcelain and pottery.

The Tokio Times, Vol. I., No. 8. Japan and Corea. 1. International communications. 2. Government and politics of Japan.

The following are the latest publications on Chinese subjects:

A Quarter of a Century in China. Shanghai, 1876.

Sketches of Excursions to Chusan, Pootoo, Nanking, and Kioto. Shanghai. 1876.

Catalogue of a Collection of Oriental Porcelain and Pottery, lent for exhibition, by A. W. Franks, F.R.S., F.S.A. London, 1876.

Grammaire de la langue Chinoise, orale et écrite. Par Paul Perny. Paris. 1876.

Tea and the Tea Trade, By Reginald Hanson, M.A. London. 1876.

Cours Graduel et Complet de Chinois. Par Comte Kleczkowski. Paris, 1876.

The Chinese Mandarin Language. After Ollendorff's Method. By Ch. Rudy. Paris, 1876.

Histoire de l'Asie Centrale (Afghanistan, Boukhara, Khiva, Khoqnand), depuis les dernières années du règne de Nadir Châh (1153) jusqu'en 1233 de l'Hégire (1740-1818). Par Mir Abdoul Kerim. Publiée, traduite et annotée par Charles Schefer. Paris, 1876.

A Narrative of the recent Events in Tong-King. With an introduction on the history and geography of Tong-King. By Henry Cordier. London, 1876.

A Chinese Dictionary in the Cantonese Dialect. By Ernest John Eitel, Ph.D. Tubing. Part I., A.—K. London, Trübner & Co.; Hongkong, Lane, Crawford & Co.; Shanghai, Kelly & Walsh, 1876.

England and China. Two Episodes of recent Anglo-Chinese History. By Justum. London, 1876.

China. A Geographical, Statistical and Political Sketch. By Alfred E. Hippisley. 1876.

NOTES AND QUERIES.

NOTES.

A CHINESE DICTIONARY IN THE CANTONESE DIALECT.—The author of this work, the first part of which has just been published, wishes to state that by an oversight he omitted to include among the names of those, to whom he expresses himself, in the preface, specially indebted for assistance and advice, the name of E. H. Parker, Esq., of H. B. M. Consular Service, the latter gentleman having placed at his disposal a copy of Dr. Williams' Tonic Dictionary containing many valuable corrections of the original, especially in the matter of tones.

"WATCHING SPIRITS" (*China Review*, Vol. v. p. 196).—The paragraph here referred to, in *The Folk-lore of China*, about "Watching Spirits," is not without foundation, though the ideas of "Watchmen of purgatory" and of the spirits in question "haunting" the persons that save life are not current here as far as I can ascertain. When a person meets with his death by any particular agency, as fire, water or wild beasts, his ghost becomes subordinated to that destroying agent and tries to insnare other victims. Till it is relieved by another ghost of one so destroyed, it cannot transmigrate.

There is a story common in street literature about a water-ghost being promoted to the tutelage of a district city (水鬼陞城隍). This water-ghost appeared in the form of a youth to a fisherman; and they became intimate friends. One night the youth came with a sad face and told the fisherman that they must part. "Don't be afraid," said he, "when I tell you that I am not a man but the ghost of one drowned in this river. To-morrow, a woman will be drowned here and take my place." Next day, sure enough the fisherman saw a woman with a babe in her arms fall into the river, and his first impulse was to rescue her, but, remembering his friend, he left her to her fate. Afterwards, to his surprise, he saw the woman escape from the water with her babe still in her arms. That night the youth also came back, and said their good-fellowship might continue. The fisherman asked for an explanation, and the youth replied, "That woman had a babe in her arms, and I could not bear to sacrifice two lives for the sake of one, so I saved her." "Then," said the fisherman, "I don't see why a humane ghost like yourself should have to wait for another to take his place before seeing again the light of the living." Some days after this the youth returned wearing a gorgeous dress and a crown. He said, Yuhwang had, on account of his unselfishly saving two lives, promoted him to the tutelage of such and such a city, where he invited his old friend to come by and by and give him a call.

The subordination of ghosts of men killed by tigers to their fierce destroyers is mentioned in *Kanghi's Dictionary* under the character 倀.

It may be that the Chinese are deterred from saving life by the fear of the vengeance of such ghosts; but I think that, in addition to callousness, the most common deterring motive is fear of the consequences of failure, not of success.

JOHN CHALMERS.

CHINESE FOLK-LORE.—Dr. Dennys, in his *Folk-lore of China*, gives on p. 11 a "formula for ascertaining the sex of a coming child." Here is another one :—

生	若	除	七
男	男	去	七
若	逢	母	四
是	單	生	十
女	位	年	九
三	若	再	問
五	女	添	娘
入	必	一	何
黃	成	十	月
泉	雙	九	有

Its meaning being as follows:— Take seven multiplied with seven, that is forty-nine. Ask the mother in what month she got pregnant, and add the number of the said month. Deduct the number of the mother's age, and add again nineteen. If the child is of the masculine sex, the number thus obtained will be an odd one; if it is of the feminine sex, it will be an even one. If according to that calculation the child ought to be a boy, and it happens to be a girl, she will die at the age of three to five.

CH. P.

YIN AND YANG, ACCORDING TO ARISTOTLE.
—The following Analysis by G. H. Lewes
of a passage from the Second Chapter of
Aristotle's Treatise on the Generation of
Animals displays the striking similarity of
Chinese and Greek speculation on the same
subject:—

"First he desires us to understand the
masculine and feminine *principles*: the masculine principle being the origin of all
motion and generation; the feminine principle being the origin of the material
generated (τὸ μὲν ἄρρεν ὡς τῆς κινήσεως καὶ τῆς
γινέσεως ἔχον τὴν ἀρχήν, τὸ δὲ θῆλυ ὡς ὕλης.) The
proof is furnished by observation as to the
origin of the sperm. It is because these
principles are secreted *from* the male and *in*
the female, that they are masculine and
feminine," for we name masculine that
which engenders in another; and feminine
that which engenders in itself. On this
account "we regard the earth as a mother,
and the heaven or sun, as the generator and
father." READER.

———

PIDGIN ENGLISH (see page 207.)—In
reply to H. L. D.'s enquiry (p. 207) ought
English to be called Fan Wá? I would say
generally speaking it might be so designated, but in a Court of Justice where
accuracy is indispensable, Ying Wa would
be more correct, both as distinguishing
English from Chinese, and also from other
European languages. Next ought Pidgin
English to be designated Ham Shui Wa?
Certainly, for the following reason. At Canton the term Ham Shui [鹹 水] is used
of things which are not correct, things which
have an inherent badness. The term is
frequently used of incorrect Kun Wa. A
man who speaks the Official dialect imper-
fectly is said to speak *Ham Shui Kun Wa*.
The idea conveyed to the Chinese mind
being expressed by the words Yam shap
陰 濕 and illustrated by the constant
presence of dampness in things which have
been saturated with sea water—they are
continually as they ought not to be. This

is the idea conveyed by the phrase and explains its suitability as a designation for
"pidgin" English. It has been suggested
that from its literal meaning *Salt water* the
use of the phrase may have arisen in connection with and as applied to Foreigners,
but for this idea there is no foundation in
fact, much as a certain objectionable use
of the term might seem at first sight to
suggest. A. B. H.

———

Your correspondent under "Queries,"
Π. L. D., asks for a reason why Pidgin
English should be called "Hám shui wá."

This term "Saltwater language" is applied by Cantonese to the peculiar dialect of
the boat population of Hongkong, which
differs from the "Punti" as spoken on shore.

It seems therefore to me, that this term
of "Hám shui wá" was not very far fetch-
ed as designating the broken English spoken
by Chinese.

J. BUSI.

———

QUERIES.

GOETHE'S "WERTHER" IN CHINA.—The
following quotations are extracted from a
standard English work on the Life and
Works of Goethe. Speaking of *Werther*,
it says: "It was the companion of Napoleon,
when in Egypt; it penetrated into China."
Again, "In the Chinese Empire, Charlotte
and Werther were modelled in porcelain."

If these quotations were not taken from
one of the most reliable of living Authors,
I should not have troubled the Readers
of the *Review*; but this being the case, it
would be interesting to trace out who was
the sympathetic soul that had the plastic
skill and artistic taste to model out Charlotte
and Werther in clay for the Chinese
workman, and whether any Werthers, or
Charlottes have been found. "Werther"
was published in 1774. Consequently it
may have been one of the employés of the
English or Dutch East India Companies
at Canton.

INQUIRER.

CHINESE MUSIC.—Has any one heard a Chinese sing or hum or beat in *triple* time? The writer has kept his attention to this point for several years in the North of China, but without hearing any but *duple* time. A more varied choice of measure may hold in the South.

S.

WHITE ANTS.—In my reading the other day I noticed a statement to the effect that white ants went through all their metamorphoses in the egg; an experience which is contrary to the nature of winged insects generally. Can any of the readers of the *China Review* refer me to a work where such an observation is scientifically recorded, or inform me whether and where the same fact has been noted by Chinese naturalists?

INQUIRER.

BOOKS WANTED, EXCHANGES, &c.

(All addresses to care of Editor, *China Review.*)

BOOKS WANTED.

Wade's Yü-yen Tsŭ-erh Chi and Key. 8 parts, second-hand or new.

Address, J. K. L.

Li-ki on *Mémorial des Rites*, traduit poue la première fois du Chinois et accompagné dr notes, de commentaires et du texte original, par J. M. Callery. Turin, 1853.

Address, H. K.

The undersigned wants a printed or manuscript copy of the following books, 島夷志畧, 安南志畧, 越史畧 and 交州記, the three first of which are mentioned in Wylie's Bibliography respectively on p. 47 and 33. He would feel greatly obliged if any readers of the *China Review* would assist him in procuring these works.

W. P. G.

TO PURCHASE OR EXCHANGE.

Endliches Verzeichniss der Chinesischen und Japanischen Münzen des K. K. Münz und Antiken-Cabinetes in Wien 1837, 8vo.

Native Treatises on Numismatics.

A Collection of Bank Notes issued by the Daimios of Japan.

Rare Chinese and Japanese Coins.

Address, A.

(Hongkong.)